BILINGUAL TENSIONS IN CANADA

Robert M. Laxer, General Editor

Associate Editors:
Wayne Jackson
Pat MacDermott

Collaborators:
Michel Allard
André Francoeur
Robert Savoie

A joint project of the Ontario Institute for Studies
in Education and the Canada Studies Foundation

Curriculum Series / 41
The Ontario Institute for Studies in Education

THE ONTARIO INSTITUTE FOR STUDIES IN EDUCATION has three prime functions: to conduct programs of graduate study in education, to undertake research in education, and to assist in the implementation of the findings of educational studies. The Institute is a college chartered by an Act of the Ontario Legislature in 1965. It is affiliated with the University of Toronto for graduate studies purposes.

The publications program of The Ontario Institute for Studies in Education has been established to make available information and materials arising from studies in education, to foster the spirit of critical inquiry, and to provide a forum for the exchange of ideas about education. The opinions expressed should be viewed as those of the contributors.

© The Ontario Institute for Studies in Education 1979
252 Bloor Street West, Toronto, Ontario M5S 1V6

All rights reserved. No part of this publication may be reproduced in any form without permission from the publisher, except for brief passages quoted for review purposes.

Canadian Cataloguing in Publication Data

Main entry under title:

Bilingual tensions in Canada
(Curriculum series ; 41)

"A joint project of the Ontario Institute for Studies in Education and the Canada Studies Foundation."

ISBN 0-7744-0183-4

1. Language question – Canada.* 2. Canada – English-French relations. 3. Bilingualism – Canada.
I. Laxer, Robert M., 1915- II. Ontario Institute for Studies in Education. III. Canada Studies Foundation. IV. Series.

JL25.B54   409'.71   C79-094685-8

ISBN 0-7744-0183-4   Printed in Canada
1 2 3 4 5 6 TO 38 28 18 08 97

CONTENTS

Preface / v
Acknowledgements / vii

1 Can Canada's Two Societies Live in One Federation? / 1
   The Problem / 1
   Learning from Past Errors / 2
   Historical Tensions between English-Speaking Canada and Quebec / 6
   Trudeau and His Plan to Save Confederation / 9
   Multiculturalism / 11
   The Language Question Crystallizes in Quebec / 12
   Reciprocity with Quebec? / 13
   The Same Problem Emerges / 14
   Report of the Pepin–Robarts Task Force on Canadian Unity / 15
   Is There a Solution? / 16

2 Why Is Language at the Heart of French–English Relations? / 20
   Quebec's Cultural Survival / 21
   The "Quiet Revolution" in Quebec / 23
   The Importance of Language to Cultural Survival / 25
   Perspectives: Language and French–English Relations / 26

3 Bilingualism in the Control Tower: The Air Traffic Control Dispute of 1976 / 31
   Background / 31
   The Air Traffic Control Dispute / 32
   Reactions to the Dispute / 35
   English Canada's Reaction / 36
   French Canada's Reaction / 38

4 Canada's Official Languages Act and Quebec's Bill 101 / 43
   The Official Languages Act, 1969 / 43
   Background to Quebec's Bill 101 / 49
   The Threat to the French Majority in Quebec / 51
   Bill 101 / 53

5 Language of Education / 56
   A Long History / 57
   Sources of Conflict / 58
   Dispute over Language of Education in Manitoba / 60
   The French Language in Ontario Schools / 62
   Unilingualism as Policy Outside Quebec / 69

6 The Winds of Assimilation: Francophones Outside Quebec / 70
   The Present Situation / 70
   Surveying the Scene / 72
   New Hope for French-Canadian Survival Outside Quebec / 90

PREFACE

"Canada and its constitutional system is in a protracted state of crisis," the Pepin-Roberts Task Force on Canadian Unity concluded in 1979 after two years of study. (The Task Force on Canadian Unity, *A Future Together: Observations and Recommendations*, Ottawa: Queen's Printer, January 1979, p. 3.) This Task Force of eight English and French Canadians was co-chaired by a former member of the Trudeau Liberal cabinet, Jean-Luc Pepin, and a former Conservative premier of Ontario, John Robarts.

In its final report, the Task Force asserted that "to confront the heart of the issue today is to address one main question, namely, the status of Quebec and its people in the Canada of tomorrow." (p. 23) The report stressed that Quebec is "distinctive" and that Canada is a "duality": a country made up primarily of two major cultural groups, English- and French-speaking Canadians.

In asserting that "Quebec is distinctive and should, within a viable Canada, have the powers necessary to protect and develop its distinctive character," the Committee recognized the importance of language as a crucial component of cultural distinctiveness. To achieve the objective of preserving Quebec's distinctiveness, the Task Force favored a reversal of the tendency of the *federal* government under Pierre Trudeau to take primary responsibility for language rights and practices. Instead, it recommended that control over language be essentially a *provincial* responsibility, except where the federal government was directly involved.

The Task Force's major recommendation on language was that "Each provincial legislature should have the right to determine an official language or official languages for that province, within its sphere of jurisdiction" and that "linguistic rights should be expressed in provincial statutes . . ." (p. 121)

The Pepin-Roberts Task Force saw *language* as the core of a people's culture. In its view, if Quebec's cultural distinctiveness was to be maintained and encouraged, Quebec would necessarily have to control most public language practices and rights. It followed too that if Quebec were to gain exclusive control over language in its area of jurisdiction and in the private sector of industry and commerce, other provinces would claim similar control.

The Task Force saw control of language by Quebec as a key to its full acceptance of a future in a federated Canada.

This book considers the role which the issue of language – particularly the use of French by French Canadians in education and in daily life – has played in Canada during the recent years, and provides descriptive and source materials on selected issues. Certain topics, for example, education in French in Manitoba and Ontario, are placed in their historical context. Particular use is made of newspaper extracts to highlight certain issues.

Chapter 1 reviews and interprets the contemporary debate over language and the status of official languages in various parts of Canada. Chapter 2 examines the relationship between language and cultural preservation and the part which language has played in the evolution of Quebec's distinctiveness and its nationalism. Chapter 3 focusses on the air traffic controllers' dispute over language in the summer of 1976, which brought the issue to a head and revealed the wide gap between the attitudes of English Canada and those of Quebec toward the role of the French language in that province, and in Canada as a whole. Chapter 4 describes the federal government's Official Languages Act of 1969 and Quebec's response, Bills 22 and 101. Chapter 5 touches on one of the most sensitive issues, the history of education in the French language in Manitoba and in Ontario. Chapter 6 deals with the question of assimilation or the possibility of the eventual disappearance of the French language outside Quebec.

While the federal policy of bilingualism has been a particular point of emphasis of the Liberal government headed by Pierre Trudeau from 1968 to 1979, the language issue was not manufactured by that government. Conflict over language policy existed long before that particular political regime and even before the political party system had evolved in its contemporary form in Canada. Whatever the political stripe of the federal government in the past, and no matter who has been prime minister, tension has existed between English-speaking and French-speaking Canadians over language rights and practices in various parts of Canada, whether it be a francophone minority outside Quebec facing an anglophone majority, or an anglophone minority in Quebec facing a majority of francophones.

There is no easy solution to the threatened future of Canada. However, it is almost axiomatic that there can be no permanent guarantee of Canada's survival without a resolution of this two-hundred-year-old conflict over language, a resolution that must involve the acceptance of the English and the French as the country's two founding peoples and its two major cultural collectivities.

As informed individuals, students of secondary schools and other institutions in English Canada can make a contribution to their society by approaching the language issue with a minimum of prejudice and a maximum of knowledge, by understanding the viewpoints of Quebeckers and other French Canadians, the other "solitude" of our country.

While language is only one of the major dimensions of French-English relations, as the Pepin-Robarts Task Force pointed out, its resolution would help create a Canadian future that would meet the needs and aspirations of its two founding peoples.

Robert M. Laxer, Project Co-ordinator and General Editor

ACKNOWLEDGEMENTS

This book is the product of a project which involved secondary school teachers in Manitoba, New Brunswick, Quebec, and Ontario from 1975 to 1977 and of which the editor served as co-ordinator. It is perhaps not accidental that these four provinces have had, historically, the greatest involvement with the issue of language in education. An earlier version of this manuscript was tested in secondary schools of these provinces by some forty teachers of history and the social sciences. The long process preceding publication included research by teachers, writing by the editor and associate editors, evaluation by teachers in classrooms, rewriting, updating with new materials, and final editing.

Bilingual Tensions in Canada was part of a larger project, "Relations and Tensions in Canada," which was sponsored and supported by the Canada Studies Foundation. The active participation of anglophone and francophone teachers was a crucial factor in the effort to achieve a balanced view of the persisting issue of language as a source of tension in Canada.

Teachers from all provinces involved contributed materials to the project: it is difficult to single out any particular teachers for special mention (a list of teachers who participated is given on the back cover). However, five people who acted as co-ordinators in their own areas made a special contribution: André Francoeur in Montreal; Wayne Jackson in Sault Ste. Marie; Dan McDevitt in Metro Toronto; Monty Szakacs in Winnipeg; and George Haley in Fredericton.

In addition, Michel Allard, professor and chairman of the Department of the Science of Education at the Université du Québec à Montréal, and Robert Savoie, a secondary school teacher in Montreal, made special contributions to the conceptualization of the project.

Officers and officials of the Canada Studies Foundation - Bob Anderson, Paul Gallagher, and Bernie Hodgetts - were very encouraging through various stages of the project. Without their support and the grants from the Foundation this publication would not have been possible.

The Ontario Institute for Studies in Education, through grants over the whole period, made possible the necessary research, writing, evaluation, editing, and, finally, publication.

While all the people mentioned (including those on the back cover) contributed to the project, the two Associate Editors of the book, Wayne Jackson and Pat MacDermott, made major contributions to the research writing and editing of the final publication.

Louise Amm, who co-ordinated the effort to track down references before publication, made it possible to meet the deadline by her persistence and calm determination.

The Editor owes a particular debt of gratitude to John McConnell of the editorial staff of OISE, whose general knowledge of Canadian history, combined with editorial skill and patience, helped to eliminate repetition and to round out the manuscript with proper references and additional materials.

Professor Roland Lamontagne of the Department of History of the University of Montreal read a pre-publication manuscript and suggested additional material.

To all who participated, and particularly to those who are mentioned by name, the editor extends grateful thanks, with the clear understanding that he bears full responsibility for major and minor changes in the final manuscript and for its shortcomings.

1
Can Canada's Two Societies Live in One Federation?

THE PROBLEM

Canadian television and newspapers have given extensive coverage to the intense debate over the future relations between English and French Canada, a debate which will ultimately determine the fate of the country. The arguments and disagreements have caused many Canadians to question the ability of Canada's political leaders to devise a framework within which the historic and contemporary interests of both French-speaking and English-speaking Canadians can be accommodated.

Will Confederation remain essentially as it has been for 110 years? Will Quebec establish a sovereign state? Can Confederation be restructured to the mutual benefit of both French and English-speaking Canadians? Put a different way, these questions become much more personal. For example: What kind of Canadian will you call yourself in the year 1985 or 1990? What would be your national identity if the country were to split apart? Would a change in Canada's structure affect your feelings toward Canada? If major changes take place, would you wish to become American? If you were a French Canadian living in Quebec today, would you call yourself a Canadian or a Québécois?

Because Canadians have such important decisions to make in the 1980s, it is necessary that each of us try to examine as objectively as possible the emotional arguments about French-English relations. If we Canadians fail to listen to each other, if we do not demonstrate an interest in reaching a compromise, we risk the emergence of hardened positions and stalemates.

To move toward a solution it is essential to recognize that answers are not easy to find and that solutions cannot be arrived at without give and take, without compromises and accommodations, without inconveniences and sacrifices.

Students can contribute to the dialogue by insisting that the national debate be focussed on issues of national survival and the common good. Together, we can insist that our political representatives be flexible and ever conscious of the need to find workable solutions. Young students, as those who will shape the future course of their country and society, should aim at becoming informed citizens.

Questions
Locate articles and excerpts from newspapers which report on the current status of English–French relations. (Among the headings to check are: "Confederation," "Bilin-

gualism," "Biculturalism," "Multiculturalism," "Nationalism," "Separatism.") Select several articles for close examination.

1. (a) Do the articles suggest that there is a serious problem concerning English-French relations? What is the nature of the problem?
   (b) Over what issues is there disagreement between the two language groups?
   (c) Can you find any evidence to suggest that Canadians in various parts of the country have different views concerning the problem?
   (d) Attempt to find a solution to the problem.

2. Write a brief summary of the articles. Be prepared to share your summary with your colleagues.

LEARNING FROM PAST ERRORS

We Canadians are now paying a heavy price for our failure to develop a consensus over vital issues which have been sources of tension between the two founding peoples — the English and the French. We have allowed numerous opportunities to pass us by when we could have created a new climate of understanding and mutual respect.

When the French in Canada were the first to call themselves "Canadiens," they were criticized for being too oriented to their own society and disloyal to the British Empire. Our most serious splits included Canada's participation in the Boer War (1899) and the use of conscription in the two world wars. The largely English-Canadian federal government forced many French Canadians to act against their will. To many English Canadians loyalty to Canada was equated with loyalty to the British Empire.

When French Canadians supported "O Canada" as our national anthem, English Canadians questioned their loyalty. By the time "God Save the King/Queen" was replaced by "O Canada," French Canadians had lost enthusiasm. A song like Gilles Vigneault's "Mon Pays" had become an unofficial national anthem for Quebec in place of "O Canada," which a now-forgotten French Canadian (Adolphe Routhier) had written in the nineteenth century.

When French Canadians proposed a distinct flag for Canada almost a century ago, English Canada continued to insist on the retention of the British Union Jack and later the Canadian Ensign (a variation of the British flag). By the time English Canada finally decided to have a Canadian flag in the 1960s, Quebeckers had adopted the fleur-de-lis as their "national" flag.

Will we miss the boat again? The next few years may see our last chance for arriving at an accommodation that will provide English Canada and Quebec with a symbiotic relationship within a general political entity called Canada.

"Mon Pays" by Gilles Vigneault.

Mon pays ce n'est pas un pays c'est
    l'hiver
Mon jardin ce n'est pas un jardin
    c'est la plaine
Mon chemin ce n'est pas un chemin
    c'est la neige

> Mon pays ce n'est pas un pays
>   c'est l'hiver
>
> *
>
> My country is not a country it's the
>   winter
> My garden is not a garden
>   it's the plain
> My road is not a road
>   it's the snow
> My country is not a country it's the
>   winter
>
>   – Refrain from "Mon Pays," avec les vieux mots (1972), Nouvelles Editions de l'Arc, Montréal. With English translation, *The Globe and Mail*, Toronto, February 7, 1973

The Globe and Mail, *Toronto, May 25, 1978*

O Canada: A Repertoire Under One Title

When a performer sings Canada's national anthem at a sports event, he has a large repertoire to choose from.

There are nearly 20 published versions of O Canada in English and one version in French. During the past week a bilingual version and another English version have come to light — much to the discontent of some English-speaking Canadians.

Roger Doucet, the man who sings the national anthem when the Montreal Canadiens play at the Forum in Montreal, drew the wrath of former Prime Minister John Diefenbaker last week when he replaced an often repeated "we stand on guard for thee" with "we stand on guard for rights and liberty."

When Mr. Doucet repeated his version at the Forum on Tuesday night, he was greeted with loud applause.

Improvisation drew a less happy response for Toronto singer Ruth Ann Wallace.

She was booed on two consecutive days last weekend by spectators at Toronto Blue Jays baseball games when she sang parts of the national anthem in French.

The Senate voted unanimously yesterday to congratulate the Blue Jays and Miss Wallace for showing their confidence in Canada's two official languages. The House of Commons voted unanimously on Tuesday to congratulate the baseball team.

Here are some of the different versions of the national anthem. The question of an official version has been on the Commons order paper for 14 years without being resolved.

The first stanza and chorus of the English version of O Canada:

> O Canada! Our home and native land!
>   True patriot love in all thy sons command.
> With glowing hearts we see thee rise,
>   The True North, strong and free,
> And stand on guard, O Canada,
>   We stand on guard for thee.
>
> O Canada, glorious and free!
>   We stand on guard, we stand on guard for thee.
> O Canada, we stand on guard for thee!

– As written for the tercentenary of Quebec in 1908 by Stanley Weir (1856-1926), recorder of Montreal and sometime judge of the Exchequer Court of Canada.

The first stanza of the French version of O Canada now is generally the only one sung:

> O Canada! terre de nos aieux,
>   Ton front est ceint de fleurons glorieux.

3

Car ton bras sait porter l'épée,
  Il sait porter la croix;
Ton histoire est une épopée
  Des plus brillants exploits;
Et ta valeur, de foi trempée,
  Protégera nos foyers et nos droits.
Protégera nos foyers et nos droits.

- As commissioned for the official visit to Quebec in 1880 of the Governor-General (the Marquess of Lorne) and Princess Louise and written by Calixa Lavallée (1842-1891), bandsman, teacher and promoter.

A translation of the French version of O Canada into English:

O Canada! Land of our ancestors,
  Your brow is girded with glorious jewels.
Because your arm knows how to carry a sword,
  It knows how to carry the cross;
Your history is an epic
  Of the most brilliant exploits;
And your valor, of tested faith,
  Will protect our homes and our rights.

The version of O Canada that was booed when sung by Ruth Ann Wallace at Exhibition Place last weekend:

O Canada! Our home and native land!
  True patriot love in all thy sons command.
Car ton bras sait porter l'épée,
  Il sait porter la croix;
Ton histoire est une épopée
  Des plus brillants exploits;

O Canada, glorious and free!
  Protégera nos foyers et nos droits.
O Canada, we stand on guard for thee!

The change made in the chorus by Roger Doucet at the two most recent Stanley Cup games in Montreal:

O Canada, glorious and free!
  We stand on guard for rights and liberty.
O Canada, we stand on guard for thee!

The Sault Star, *Sault Sainte Marie, Ontario, May 24, 1978*
Reprinted with permission of The Canadian Press

Booing of Anthem "Sad Commentary"

OTTAWA (CP) - Prime Minister Trudeau said Tuesday the booing of the singing of O Canada in French at a Toronto baseball game Sunday was "a sad commentary" that showed many Canadians still do not realize the importance of the French language in the country.

But Trudeau told his weekly news conference that there was little that could be done about it except continue to sing in both languages until people "slowly attune their ears to the reality that there are two languages in Canada and two main linguistic groups."

"This is a political and social reality that is not perceived well in every part of the country," he said. "Hopefully this kind of incident will further the education and cause a correction of that kind of booing."

He said the booing could be used by the Parti Quebecois to convince French-speaking Quebecers that they are not welcome in Canada and should separate.

Trudeau said his government has developed its official languages policy, to provide services in French and English across the country, to counter the separatist argument that there should be a French-speaking area separate from the rest of Canada.

Earlier, the Commons voted unanimously to congratulate the Toronto Blue Jays baseball club for playing O Canada in both official languages during the weekend.

All members supported a motion from Toronto Liberal David Collenette (York East) that the club be congratulated for demonstrating "confidence in a unified Canada and in both official languages."

MPs applauded the motion after it was passed.

The vote followed a telegram sent to the club

by 15 Toronto MPs with much the same message.

Sunday and Monday Toronto fans booed when the national anthem was sung in French.

The telegram, from 12 Liberals, two Progressive Conservatives and one New Democrat, said:

"All the undersigned elected federal members of Parliament from Metropolitan Toronto commend the Toronto Blue Jays organization and team for its presentation of Canada's national anthem during its games in Toronto over the Victoria Day weekend. We share your pride in our country and your recognition of both official languages."

The Globe and Mail, *Toronto, May 22, 1978*

Blue Jay Fans Boo French Words in Anthem

Fans booed when singer Ruth Anne Wallace sang part of O Canada in French before the start of yesterday's double-header between Toronto Blue Jays and New York Yankees at Exhibition Stadium.

Miss Wallace, 26, formerly of Simcoe, said she expected some booing but not as much as there was while she sang in French.

It was the fifth time the bilingual singer had sung O Canada at a Blue Jays game, but the first time she sang it in both languages.

"It didn't bother me that much, though — there was some clapping," she said later.

Miss Wallace said she had been wanting to sing in both French and English at the games and yesterday Blue Jays' management consented to the bilingual rendition.

"I did it for Canadian unity, which is more important than ever."

She said that if the Toronto club agrees, she will sing the bilingual version before today's American League game between Toronto and Boston.

Peter Durso, Blue Jays' promotions director, said the club will make a decision before the game.

The Globe and Mail, *Toronto, February 22, 1978*
Reprinted with permission of The Canadian Press

Quebeckers Start Competition to Find National Anthem of Own

MONTREAL (CP) - The Quebec nationalist St. Jean Baptiste Society has organized a competition to find 10 "national songs" with the hope that the most popular will become Quebec's anthem.

When the group unveiled details of the competition Monday, one of its members suggested a variation of the French-language version of O Canada, substituting O Quebec for O Canada.

Jean-Claude Champagne, president of the group's Montreal chapter, replied with a smile that he didn't see any reason why that could not be submitted.

Although Stanley Weir's English lyrics to O Canada are clearly pan-Canadian, the earlier French lyrics by Sir Adolphe Routhier do not contain phrases such as "from sea to shining sea," and are overwhelmingly religious in tone.

For example, the last refrain of the fourth verse ends the anthem with a ringing call to repeat "like our fathers, the vanquishing cry, 'For Christ and the King.' "

An application form says the contest is to give Quebec "songs that reflect the Quebecois reality and create a sense of belonging to a country, a nation.

"From the first repertory of quality material there will perhaps come a song that will quickly become a rallying point of our people, an object of our pride and a sign of our determination."

The 10 finalists will get $500 each.

* * *

Questions

1. Why are French and English Canadians referred to as "founding peoples"? Do you agree that these ethnic groups are entitled to a "special" position or status in contemporary Canada?

2. To what extent would your neighbors accept the idea of the English and the French as the two "founding peoples" of Canada?

3. To what extent did each of the following generate bitterness between English and French Canadians?
    Boer War, 1899.
    Conscription Crisis, 1917.
    Conscription Crisis, 1944.

4. Why might some Canadians assume that "being Canadian" is the same as being loyal to Britain?

5. Research the background to the Union Jack. What is its history? How representative of Canada was the Union Jack in the early 1960s? (You might wish to examine the population data for Canada in 1961.)

6. Why do you suppose symbols are important to our lives? Can you give examples of "symbols"?

7. Vigneault once described "Mon Pays" as a song which "seeks identification but finds none." How important do you feel it is that people have a strong sense of national identity?

HISTORICAL TENSIONS BETWEEN ENGLISH-SPEAKING CANADA AND QUEBEC

Tensions have existed between English and French Canadians since the defeat of French forces in North America in 1759. Following the "conquest," English-speaking Canadians made many attempts to impose a British character on Canada.

Abolition of French as a recognized language in Canada was perceived as the key to the assimilation of the French.

Lord Durham's report of 1839 was only the best known of many serious attempts to make English the sole official language of communication. (The activities of the Orange Order in this regard and their virulent anti-French campaigns of the last years of the nineteenth century and the years prior to World War I provide another example of such attempts.) Yet Durham's proposal and those of others with similar views were never fully realized, at least in Quebec, for two main reasons. First, French Canadians were determined that their culture and their language would survive despite all obstacles. Second, there were English Canadians who foresaw that the destruction of French in British North America would necessitate a devastating civil war with a ruthless dispersal of French-speaking Canadians out of Quebec, as happened with the Acadians in the Maritimes in 1755. And even such extreme measures would not necessarily assure the elimination of the French language, as the Acadians have proven by their vigorous come-back in New Brunswick, two centuries after they were supposedly annihilated as a cultural group.

The question of the French language has always been at the heart of French-Canadian survival in an English-speaking North America. Much of the tension between English Canada and Quebec over the past two centuries has focussed on the language question. It is in the centre of the present debate over Canada's future, and has consequently been selected as the focus of this work.

While the most extreme advocates of French assimilation did not prevail as far as Quebec itself was concerned, the moves to assimilation in Canada outside Quebec were much more successful. An early example was Manitoba's abolition of public support for French-language schools in 1890; another was Ontario's Instruction (Regulation) 17 passed in 1912. Until recently, with the sole exception of New Brunswick, all other English-speaking provinces have ignored the demands of their francophones for province-wide public French-language schooling, such as Quebec has always provided for its anglophones.

The guiding policy that underlay these actions in denying educational and other language rights to French Canadians outside Quebec — rights equal to those of English Canadians in Quebec — was that Canada was and ought to remain English-speaking. Schools outside Quebec were to be "national" schools with English as the language of instruction; Quebec was to be a recognized exception to the rule. Quebec was to be bilingual, while the rest of Canada would be unilingual.

After 1945 there emerged in Quebec a challenge to the permanence of the French language as the language of the majority. This was not by means of a direct challenge to constitutional principles; the threat originated as a result of mass immigration.

Between 1867 and 1941 people of British extraction had always constituted over 55 percent of Canada's population and those of French origin about 30 percent. The remaining 10 to 15 percent were made up of people from dozens of countries — mainly of European descent. They included, too, people of Asian and African extraction as well as the native peoples — the Indians and Innuit — who were here long before the Old World explorers arrived in the sixteenth century. In general, about 70 percent of Canadians spoke English and about 30 percent spoke French.

In the 1950s the relative ratio of French to English began to change. In 1978, just as at the time of Confederation, there were still only two major linguistic groups with an historically evolved character. However, a third component, made up of nonanglophone people from over a hundred countries and all continents, had begun to change the balance between English-speaking and French-speaking Canadians, so that by 1978 the ethnic make up of the country was as follows: people of British origin, 46 percent; people of French origin, 26 percent; all others, 28 percent.

Canadians of British origin continue to constitute the largest cultural bloc in Canada. They have a history extending through many centuries that includes a common origin in the British Isles — England, Ireland, Scotland, and Wales — and shared traditions and experiences. As a community, they have had a continuous presence in North America for over three hundred years. Since the early nineteenth century, the English-speaking community has increased largely as a result of immigration from the British Isles. This group, comprising less than one-half the population of Canada, has influence far beyond its numbers. The vast majority of nonanglophone immigrants who have come to Canada in the past one hundred and fifty years have gravitated to the English-Canadian community, adopting English as their language. Those who immigrated to Canada in the period following World War II have, by exercising their language choice, swelled the size of the anglophone community both within Quebec and within the country at large.

Descendants of immigrants have within one generation invariably mastered the English language more fully than the language of their forebears. Canadian-born offspring of most nonanglophone, nonfrancophone immigrants have become integrated into the English-speaking community.

The B. and B. Commission had shown that:

> ... nine out of ten people of French origin retain French as their mother tongue; those of other origins tend progressively to adopt English.... Of those who changed languages, 93% are English-speaking today.
>
> – *Report of the Royal Commission on Bilingualism and Biculturalism*, Book I: The Official Languages (Ottawa: Queen's Printer, 1967), p. 22

As a consequence, the English-speaking community, consisting of all who speak and use English in their daily life, now constitutes almost 75 percent of the total population.

The other historically formed community consists of French-speaking Canadians. Their history in Canada can be traced to the founding of Quebec City in 1608 and of Montreal in 1642. The significance of the past to French Canadians is suggested by the fact that the vast majority of the almost six million French-speaking Canadians are descendants of the seventy thousand inhabitants of New France at the time of the Conquest in 1759. Since that time, there has been relatively little immigration from France to increase the size of the French-Canadian population.

In addition, the rate of natural increase has contributed to the decrease in the proportion of the population which can be identified as French. Formerly among the highest birth rates in the industrialized world, French Canadians, after World War II, had a natural birth rate below the Canadian average. The French-speaking community in Canada now constitutes about 25 percent of the total population, a drop of about 20 percent from 1945. The significance of the rate of natural increase to the francophone community is suggested by the following obituary. A local French-language newspaper praised the virtues of a man from Beauce County who left some six hundred descendants after his death at the age of ninety-six:

> The grandfather of Mr. Philippon met an honorable death at the Battle of the Plains of Abraham; his grandson has well revenged his death by adding, through his own [*sic!*] efforts, an entire parish to French Canada.
>
> – quoted in Richard J. Joy, *Languages in Conflict: The Canadian Experience*, Carleton Library, No. 61 (Toronto: McClelland and Stewart, 1972), p. 51

It is evident from this brief description that Canadians of nonanglophone, nonfrancophone origin, while they are more numerous than those of French origin, constitute a group only in terms of classification. Unlike English or French Canada, the "all others" category, consisting of over a hundred ethnic groups, is not an historically evolved, self-sufficient, and autonomous community. Members of this category tend to identify with and become integrated into the two major communities. Even the largest of these ethnic groups — Italian, German, or Ukrainian — is only between one-fifth and one-tenth as large as the francophone community in Canada. In terms of fluency in the language of origin, the size of any ethnic group is much smaller than that — less than one-tenth and less than one-thirtieth the size of the francophone and the anglophone communities respectively.

The implications in the changing character of the population of Canada were serious for Quebec — the homeland of the French language in Canada. The preference shown by immigrants settling in Quebec for English and English-language schooling for their children resulted in an increase in the relative size of Quebec's anglophone community. Montreal was the centre for most immigration to Quebec and it was in this metropolis, with a 60 percent francophone population, that the threat to the status of French as the language of the majority was felt most acutely by francophone Quebeckers. With a population of 2.5 million, it would have required an immigration of only thirty thousand to forty thousand a year to convert Montreal into a predominantly anglophone city by the year 2000. Given such a trend, could the province itself retain its distinctive French character?

In response to this threat of eventual assimilation, francophone Quebeckers have become more nationalistic than ever. In the 1960s Quebec nationalism began to move toward a position now described as "sovereignty-association," that is, toward a revision of Quebec's relationship with the rest of Canada. Quebec, it was argued, must have possession of complete legislative power to guarantee its survival as a nation and a culture while yet maintaining its economic links with the other provinces. This proposal brought about a sharp polarization of sentiment among francophone Quebeckers. Two people emerged as representative of conflicting approaches to the future: Pierre Elliott Trudeau and René Lévesque.

Questions
1. Define "assimilation." Why might the abolition of language rights be an effective method of assimilating a minority culture into that of the majority?
2. To what extent do you find evidence in the newspapers to support the claim that language is the main cause of division between the English and the French in Canada?
3. For what reasons might it be claimed that the United Empire Loyalists introduced a tradition which reinforced attachment to Britain?
4. Define nationalism. Give a brief description of the Acadian expulsion.
5. Discuss whether or not there is an English-speaking Canadian nationalism or identity in present-day Canada.
6. Locate in your school library biographies of Pierre Elliott Trudeau and René Lévesque and give a brief outline of the life and career of each man.

TRUDEAU AND HIS PLAN TO SAVE CONFEDERATION

Some observers have claimed that Pierre Trudeau became Prime Minister of Canada in 1968 by taking a strong stand against the new Quebec nationalism represented by René Lévesque and the Parti Québécois. Trudeau argued that official recognition of the two languages — French and English — across Canada would be a major step toward solving the historic problem of discrimination against the French in Canada.

Such a languages policy would encourage the Québécois to feel at home all over Canada by providing francophones outside Quebec with rights similar to those enjoyed by the English minority in Quebec. Trudeau challenged the nationalists and separatists of the PQ, who argued that Quebec was a nation separate from English Canada and should therefore possess the full powers of sovereignty, that is, the right to make major political, social, economic, and cultural decisions for itself. In sharp contrast to this two-nation concept of Canada, Trudeau asserted the existence of one Canadian nation within which the two historic linguistic groups would be accommodated.

Pierre Trudeau argued that the extension of language rights to the French throughout Canada would negate the nationalists' central perception of Canada as a country of two nations. Thus, between 1968 and 1976 he shifted the debate in English Canada away from the "two-nations" concept of Canada and "special status" for Quebec.

Trudeau's broad appeal in 1968 reflected in part the belief of English Canadians that his bilingualism policy would silence Quebec nationalist opposition. Trudeau had promised that equal access to the services of the federal government by English and French Canadians across Canada would keep Quebec in its place and within confederation.

After the passage of the Official Languages Act in 1969, federal government services across Canada became increasingly available in French as well as in English: numerous French TV and radio stations were opened by the CBC, and some civil servants became bilingual. However, there was no similar pace in areas under provincial control. The English-speaking provinces continued to reject demands for the use of French as one of two languages of instruction and communication in their school systems. English Canada was not prepared to embrace federal or provincial bilingualism. To do so in both federal and provincial areas would have signified acceptance of French as an official language at all levels in the country — in the schools, in the courts, in the legislatures, and in all government services. By the time of the federal elections of 1972 and 1974, English Canada had been lulled into believing that "separatism is dying or dead" in Quebec, a statement that Trudeau repeated, especially after the October Crisis of 1970. Attacks on the federal government's bilingualism policy became more open and widespread in English Canada, particularly in the West.

A new anti-French backlash, which had been mounting in the early 1970s and which was evident in the election campaign in 1972, reached its height in the Air Traffic Control dispute of 1976. English Canada overwhelmingly backed controllers and pilots in their demand that air control over Quebec be restricted to the English language. English was to be the language over Quebec air, even though Quebec's Bill 22 had made French the official language of the province, and the federal Official Languages Act had made French an official language across Canada.

Anti-French letters poured into the press. At its height very few English-Canadian spokesmen of any of the three major political parties supported French as a viable language over Quebec's air fields. This happened in spite of the acceptance of the Official Languages Act in 1969 by all three political parties.

The split was shown even in the federal Liberal cabinet itself. Francophone Jean Marchand resigned to protest the weakness of the Trudeau government in applying its own bilingual policy. At the other end of the pole was the anglophone Manitoban James Richardson, who resigned three months later because recognition of French had, in his opinion, gone too far.

Marchand and Richardson, who had been in the same Liberal cabinet for eight years under Pierre Trudeau, demonstrated the polarization over the idea of two national collectivities in Canada. Marchand recognized this as a fact of life, that Quebec was a society different from that of English Canada. Richardson would not accept this as something to be recognized permanently in the form of constitutional guarantees to francophone Quebeckers.

Questions
1. "Nationalism" and "separatism" appear to be similar forces in the Quebec context. Attempt a definition of "nationalism." What conditions must exist if a people are to be able to express their nationalism?
2. To what extent could Canada accommodate French-Canadian nationalism?
3. Can you find any evidence of an English-Canadian nationalism? If so, what identifying characteristics does it possess?
4. View the National Film Board films "The October Crises 1970: Action" and "Reaction." Identify the varieties of nationalist expression reflected in the films.

MULTICULTURALISM

One more important facet of Pierre Trudeau's policy should be noted, namely, multiculturalism. Multiculturalism, which some saw as complicating and confusing the policy of bilingualism and biculturalism, was enunciated by the federal government in 1971. In some important ways it replaced biculturalism, which had been promoted by the government of Lester Pearson. Biculturalism had been featured prominently in the famous Royal Commission on Bilingualism and Biculturalism, which issued its findings between 1965 and 1969, during most of which period Lester Pearson was Prime Minister. Biculturalism and bilingualism had emphasized the existence of two basic cultures in Canada, associated with the history and heritage of Canada's two founding peoples and their continuing role in contemporary Canada.

*Multi*culturalism shifted the focus from *bi*culturalism toward a multi-ethnic description of Canada. Through the new policy, the federal government would help all ethnic groups preserve their cultural heritage in the wider cultural and linguistic environment of Canada.

The concept of multiculturalism tended to reinforce a view of Canada held by many English-speaking Canadians. French Canadians, it was argued, are just one of the many nonanglophone ethnic communities in Canada — even though by far the largest. Popularization of multiculturalism resulted not only in federal government support for ethnic groups in their efforts to preserve their traditions, but also in its substitution for the 1960s concept of biculturalism. As a consequence, multiculturalism complemented Pierre Trudeau's downplaying of Quebec as the only home of French Canadians in Canada.

French Quebec was not to be regarded as different from that of any other ethnic group in its historic role in the past and in its potential role in the future. The attitude that Quebec was just another province and French Canadians just another ethnic group was used by the Parti Québécois to increase nationalist sentiment in Quebec. The success of the Parti Québécois in the Quebec election of November 15, 1976, showed how powerfully this nationalist feeling had been building among francophone Quebeckers.

Questions
1. To what extent can one recognize the special status of the French and the English as the two "founding peoples" while simultaneously promoting multiculturalism?

THE LANGUAGE QUESTION CRYSTALLIZES IN QUEBEC

Many Quebeckers, even before Pierre Trudeau became Prime Minister in 1968, decided that Québécois culture and nationhood could not be protected by official bilingualism or any other concession which English Canada might reluctantly make to the French. As a result, Quebec nationalists formed several political groupings and eventually the Parti Québécois (PQ) in 1968. By 1976, the year of the Parti Québécois victory in the Quebec elections, the federal Official Languages policy, which had been in operation since 1969, had not been successful in eliminating century-old grievances relating to the provision of access to French in English-speaking parts of Canada.

Even in Quebec the trend among immigrants to educate their children in English continued. Bill 22, adopted by the Quebec Liberal government of Robert Bourassa in 1974, held hope for some Quebeckers that this trend could be checked. The Bill, by making French the official language of Quebec, as English was the official language in the other provinces, was designed to halt the erosion of the French-speaking majority in Quebec. Among its provisions was the stipulation that immigrant children who did not speak fluent English must attend schools in which French would be the language of communication and instruction.

With the passage of Bill 22, Quebec had moved closer to the basic unilingual policies of other provinces. At the same time, special consideration was given to the historically established anglophone minority in Quebec and its right to educate its children in the English language.

Many Quebec nationalists, however, felt that Bill 22 had not gone far enough to guarantee their long-term survival as a cultural community. In the aftermath of the air traffic control dispute in 1976 (discussed in detail in chapter 3), in which English Canada was perceived to oppose the equality of the French language, even over the air of Quebec, Quebeckers turned to the PQ in larger numbers than before. The day the PQ was put into power — November 15, 1976 — was to be a turning point in Quebec and Canadian history.

The debate over language status was further intensified in 1977 by the PQ's language bill. Bill 101 (1977) continued the trend, begun by Bill 22, toward making French the official language of Quebec. A fierce debate raged in Montreal between anglophones and francophones over the legislation. The issue was whether educational rights would be determined primarily by collective or individual needs. What was to take precedence: the needs of the *collectivity* of five million people of francophone Quebec to survive as a national-cultural society, or the *individual right* of all Quebeckers to choose between English and French for the education of their children?

The conflict between collective and individual rights split the country. Most Quebeckers emphasized the former while most English Canadians supported the latter.

The split which had existed in the past over language and constitutional issues deepened between English Canada and Quebec. Quebec had spoken many times previously as a national collectivity (this "national" consciousness had even reached the point of renaming the Quebec legislative assembly the "National Assembly" in the 1960s), even though many English Canadians did not recognize it as such. The debate about whether any form of Canadian federation was possible had now begun.

The movement toward Quebec independence or "sovereignty-association" gathered momentum after November 15, 1976. The concept was more than an ideal to be debated; it was now official Quebec government policy. The confrontation would continue until a new constitutional framework emerged for Canada. One thing was certain, matters could not continue in their present form.

It was apparent that there was a growing chasm between English and French Canadians. Evidence of the tension was present in the debate over the federal government's Official Languages Act of 1969 and the debates over Quebec's successive language Acts — Bill 63 in 1969, Bill 22 in 1974, and Bill 101 in 1977 — and the sharp differences over language in the air traffic control dispute of 1976.

Meanwhile, other provinces, which were still unilingual, had begun to give some recognition to the educational needs of their French minorities. Yet, even in the late 1970s, these steps were not nearly as extensive as opportunities which anglophones in Quebec had enjoyed for two centuries.

Questions
1. For what reasons did the government of Robert Bourassa introduce Bill 22?
2. Do you approve or not of a government restricting the freedom of its citizens to choose the language in which their children would be educated? Give reasons for your answer.
3. Give examples of situations in which the issue of language rights appears to involve a conflict between individual rights and collective rights.

RECIPROCITY WITH QUEBEC?

It was in this climate of increased tension between English and French Canada that a meeting of Canada's ten premiers took place in St. Andrews, New Brunswick, in August 1977. Among the items on their agenda was the issue of education rights for Canada's two official language groups.

Quebec had suggested to the other nine provinces that a "reciprocity" agreement might be reached in this area. By means of a bilateral agreement with Quebec, each of the nine provinces would remain basically unilingual, but would grant minority language rights in education equivalent to those which Quebec was granting to their anglophones in Bill 101. In return, this would guarantee that anglophone children from other provinces who had at least one parent with schooling in English would be accepted into the English school system in Quebec. Such an acceptance by Quebec would be dependent on the English-speaking provinces providing similar guarantees of French schooling for francophone Quebeckers who moved into their provinces.

However, two objections discouraged and ultimately prevented such a reciprocal arrangement. First, there was the argument of the then Prime Minister, Pierre Trudeau. In advance of the August '77 conference he warned the anglophone premiers that they would be falling into the trap of the Parti Québécois if they signed any bilateral agreement with Quebec, no matter how reasonable it sounded. To do that would be setting a precedent for Quebec to sign other bilateral agreements. Signing such an agreement with the Quebec government, the argument ran, would jeopardize national unity because the PQ government could then declare to its own citizens that a movement toward "association" with English Canada was possible. Better to turn down what appeared like a reasonable proposition now than risk a split in the country later. Trudeau's solution was to stipulate, in a revised federal constitution, that anglophones and francophones in all parts of Canada had a right to education in either of the two official languages.

In addition, the English premiers raised a strong objection to Quebec's reciprocity proposal. It was argued that the agreement would make a distinction among citizens in their provinces — those who had received an English-language education and those who had not.

Children of parents educated in English-speaking countries could attend English schools if they moved to Quebec, while those whose parents were educated in nonanglophone countries would automatically be enrolled in francophone schools.

As a result, the nine English-Canadian premiers rejected Quebec's reciprocal offer. Rather than sign a formal agreement they declared, for the first time in Canadian history, that the provinces would attempt to implement French-language education for francophones in their provinces wherever feasible. René Lévesque refused to sign this document. To Lévesque it was just another "promise" without any guarantees that francophones from Quebec would receive better treatment in other provinces than they had in the past.

While the nine premiers pointed to real and perhaps insurmountable difficulties with Quebec's proposal, they did not suggest to Quebec that modification in the terms of the agreement might be acceptable. Instead they flatly rejected the proposal as unacceptable in principle. They would not be coerced into guaranteeing French-language education to their minorities; they would do it of their own free will.

The nine premiers split with Lévesque basically because they started from different premises about the nature of Quebec, namely, whether Quebec is a national collectivity or society distinct from the rest of Canada. If it is a national collectivity, it has the right to plan for its national and linguistic survival; if it is not a national collectivity, it is simply the largest nonanglophone ethnic community in Canada, which must take its chance for survival along with the dozens of smaller ethnic groups.

THE SAME PROBLEM EMERGES

The English-speaking premiers did not accept Quebec's claim that it is a genuine national collectivity. If written guarantees of French-Canadian rights were to be made, it was assumed that they would come through a revised federal constitution, as Pierre Trudeau suggested before and after the St. Andrews meeting. Such a constitutional amendment would guarantee the right to French education for those francophones who wanted it; at the same time it would uphold the right of every individual, regardless of origin, to an education in either English or French.

Here we were back to the basic difference in principle between the two cultural collectivities. There seemed to be two possibilities: either collective rights would have to supersede individual rights where one of the two national collectivities deemed its national survival to be involved — as with Quebec — or Canada was to be viewed as one nation, which would guarantee all its individual citizens choice and access to either official language, regardless of the consequences to the national survival of either collectivity as seen by Quebec.

The English-speaking premiers gave priority to the principle of the individual rights of all Canadians across Canada to choose one of the two official languages for their education. In addition, the needs of French Canadians in Quebec and elsewhere would be met where sufficient numbers warranted education in French. This was coupled with an acceptance of official bilingualism in federal institutions. However, it was assumed that English would be the working language of nine provinces while Quebec would remain fully bilingual. The statement they issued in St. Andrews was historic in that the nine anglophone premiers promised an education in French to francophones in their provinces, wherever feasible. However, although their move went beyond stipulations of the BNA Act, it was more of a *practical* concession to meet the country's crisis than an acceptance of the *right* of one of the two founding peoples to long-term national and cultural survival.

Premier Lévesque, on the other hand, worked on the principle that Quebec, as the homeland of French Canadians, required a guarantee of survival; once that was established, there could be concessions to the historic traditions of anglophones in Quebec. Collective rights of the minority Quebec "nation" would guarantee rights to the individuals of that "nation"; but collective rights of francophones would not eliminate, but only modify, the individual rights of those anglophones in Quebec who had a historic claim to such rights. This right would not, however, apply to future immigrants. Such immigrants would know the conditions for settling in Quebec in advance.

The basic differences in principle over language rights extended to the even broader political, economic, and constitutional debate over whether the two national collectivities could continue to co-exist in our country.

On the one hand was the relatively fixed position of Pierre Trudeau and his Liberal party that Confederation and the bilingualism policy since 1969, in spite of some shortcomings, had done well for Quebec. According to this position, federalism was moving in the right direction, even if too slowly.

On the other hand, there was the equally rigid position of René Lévesque and the PQ, which argued that since Confederation Quebeckers had been economically and culturally oppressed. Quebec nationalists held little stock in the old federation. English Canada, they argued, would never accept Quebec as a full and equal national collectivity within a "federal" structure. Quebec's future could be assured only with political sovereignty. The only desirable long-term arrangement they would consider was an economic association with English Canada — in line with the original meaning of the word "confederation." This idea they combined in the two words "sovereignty-association."

With what appeared to be two immovable positions facing each other, there seemed little hope for a solution. Although the St. Andrews conference showed that leaders in English Canada were still resistant to the concept of Quebec as a national collectivity, it also demonstrated that anglophones were ready to consider practical solutions. At a meeting in September 1977, the ten provincial ministers of education elected Quebec Vice-Premier Jacques Yvan Morin as chairman of their permanent council. At that meeting they decided to examine the status of English and French in the educational systems of each of the ten provinces.

The question now was, was it possible for English Canada to accept Quebec as a national collectivity while at the same time seek a compromise solution which would retain a form of Canadian political structure that would meet the needs of both founding peoples and of the more recent immigrants? Would most Quebeckers accept a compromise that would guarantee them full rights and opportunities to determine freely the future of their society, but would fall short of political separation from Canada?

REPORT OF THE PEPIN-ROBARTS TASK FORCE ON CANADIAN UNITY

In January 1979, the Task Force on Canadian Unity brought down its report. *A Future Together: Observations and Recommendations* is the first of three publications by the Task Force. The report, which resulted from a two-year study by an eight-person commission headed by John Robarts, former Conservative premier of Ontario, and Jean-Luc Pepin, a former federal Liberal minister in Pierre Trudeau's government, emphasized the "duality" of Canada. It showed that there was hope that English Canadians would move to an acceptance of Quebec as a distinct cultural society. "Let us put our conviction strongly," the Commissioners stated in *A Future Together*, "Quebec is distinctive and should, within a viable Canada, have the powers necessary to protect and develop its distinctive character; any political solution short of this would lead to the rupture of Canada." (p.87) The commissioners also recommended that "each provincial legislature should have the right to determine an official language or official languages for that province, within its sphere of jurisdiction." (p.121) It also recommended that "linguistic rights should be expressed in provincial statutes . . ." and that should "all provinces agree on these or any other linguistic rights, these rights should then be entrenched in the constitution." (pp. 121-22)

In emphasizing Quebec's "distinctive" character and the "duality" of Canada, the Pepin–Robarts Report appealed to English Canada to move toward an acceptance of Quebec's view of itself as a national collectivity. In explaining the report, John Robarts urged English Canada not to get hung up over the idea of "special status" for Quebec, because Quebec already had "special status in its legal code." Special status, he emphasized, is not the same as special "privilege."

In acknowledging that Canadian "duality is many-sided," the Task Force Report insisted "that to confront the heart of the issue today is to address *one main question, namely, the status of Quebec and its people in the Canada of tomorrow*." (p. 23) "Duality," as the dominant characteristic of Canada, means the recognition of English Canada and of Quebec as two distinct societies. The first of three questions that the Task Force set out to answer was: "How do we secure the fuller expression of *duality* in all the spheres to which it relates?"

In asserting that "Canada and its constitutional system is in a protracted state of crisis — which requires a rapid and determined response," the Task Force recognized that the time for expressing Canada's duality in a more satisfactory constitutional form was short.

IS THERE A SOLUTION?

"Canada and its constitutional system *is* in a protracted state of crisis" (p.3), said the Pepin–Robarts Task Force. Yet there is no single solution which will accommodate every demand. Any federal structure, no matter how reconstituted or amended, would be a delicate organism. Such an organism could be destroyed if any of the partners became too disenchanted or frustrated, or if the tension between them was allowed to reach the breaking point.

The test of statesmanship on both sides of Canada's "duality" will be to negotiate with great skill and sensitivity; to identify compromises which, while allowing French and English Canadians to emphasize and realize their strategic objectives, will link one to the other in a shared future.

There is a need to bring together, in a supremely creative fashion, the two fundamental democratic principles which are enshrined in the Charter of the United Nations: the *right* of the *individual* to dignity, respect, and freedom of choice and opportunity; and, the *right of nations* and *national communities* to self-determination, free from external interference or coercion. In the Canadian context this requires the recognition of the rights of every individual Canadian and the recognition of Canada's national cultural duality.

If Canadians can realize a combination of these principles, then the future could be assured. The weight of our errors of the past is such that this could be our last chance to meet Quebec halfway.

* * *

The following chapters deal primarily with the question of language, as it affects French–English relations and the search for a balance between individual rights and the rights of national collectivities. However, the language issue is only one dimension of the complex and broad theme involving French and English in Canada. Additional sources of conflict include regional and economic disparities, and differences in values and attitudes characteristic of Canadians throughout Canada.

In the examination of the issues presented in this and other chapters, one major question should be kept in mind: Why? In coming to conclusions, the facts should be collected and organized first; then you can test the reasonableness of your conclusions. The preliminary conclusions made at the end of chapter 2, for example, could be compared with those reached at the end of chapters 3 and 4.

1. FAREWELL TO ENGLISH CANADA
   "... It is about time someone told the Quebeckers that sure, they can keep their culture, but by God Canada is an English-speaking country and if they want to make it here they have got to speak English. Any other policy cooked up by soft-headed liberals will result in, and is resulting in, the disintegration of Canada."

   – Letter to the Editor, *Quest; Canada's Urban Magazine*, May 1977, p. 44

2. NATIONAL PETTINESS
   "Why hang on to a Confederation which has succeeded in kindling such animosity, such jealousy, such misunderstandings between the provinces? ... I am baffled by those who affirm loudly 'Let's all be Canadians' and spend most of their time criticizing other Canadians. To be a 'Canadian first' in minds of many English-Canadians does not mean to be united to serve Canada's interest, but to say 'zut' to Quebec!"

   – Solange Chaput-Rolland, *My Country, Canada or Quebec?* (Toronto: Macmillan, 1966), p. 22

3. FEDERALISM
   "A federal system of government is always and everywhere subject to powerful forces making for instability. This form of government is the outcome of a compromise between substantial differences based on language, religion, race, economics, or geography; and important similarities based on significant common interests. Consequently, federal systems are constantly confronted with the difficult task of working out new compromises and new accommodations between special interests and common goals."

   – J. Deutsch, introduction to R. M. Burns, ed., *One Country or Two?* (Montreal: McGill–Queen's University Press, 1979), pp. 3-4

The Toronto Star, *October 9, 1976*
Reprinted with permission – The Toronto Star

4. 'There's Still Hope for This Country'

WINNIPEG

The odd thing about the bilingual backlash is that it is directed against the federal government, Prime Minister Pierre Trudeau and Quebec, but on a one-to-one basis the average westerner will rarely show open hostility towards a French Canadian.

In two weeks of travels through the provinces of Manitoba, Saskatchewan, Alberta and British Columbia I was never once personally made to feel unwelcome.

This tends to confirm the feeling of most experts and unity watchers that there is still hope for this country if people can somehow communicate with each other.

Tone down

In other words, the situation hasn't yet deteriorated to the point where dialogue between the two cultures is impossible. But unless drastic measures are taken by the federal government to immediately tone down the hysteria of the linguistic debate, we may soon find ourselves on a headlong course towards self-destruction.

In the early '70s, politicians in Ottawa were fond of saying that even if the separatists took power, Quebec's independence could only be ratified by a national referendum. Now, however that argument has been relegated to the scrap heap.

Ottawa realizes that if a refendum were held tomorrow, a dangerously high number of Canadians would respond with a loud and clear "Yes!" to the prospect of Quebec's withdrawal from Confederation.

Where did Prime Minister Pierre Trudeau, whom many thought would go to Ottawa to save Confederation from the clutches of separatists, go wrong, and how did he manage to bring the country to the brink of constitutional collapse?

The fact is that after he introduced the Official Languages Act in 1969, he failed dismally to follow through with a mammoth sales pitch to make the legislation palatable in the West.

The result is that today a number of people in Manitoba, Saskatchewan, Alberta and British Columbia see the legislation as an attempt to force them to learn French or to "ram French down our throats."

Trudeau exhibited a short-coming common among intellectuals: He failed to realize that the average citizen doesn't think; he reacts emotionally to anything new or different.

The introduction of the Official Languages Act was so badly handled that people lost sight of the fact that the act was designed to enable French Canadians to be served in their language in federal offices coast to coast.

It was the failure to comprehend this most basic fact that leads people like Dave Parrott of St. Pierre, Man., to claim: "My understanding of it is that a French guy can come into my general store and demand to be served in French. If I can't do it, I'm breaking the law."

Or a George Ferguson of Abbotsford, B.C. who says: "Trudeau's main objective is to make French the number one language in this country. It's been one of his goals since he took office and we're not going to buy that."

If Ottawa wants to sell bilingualism in the West — and time is fast running out — it has to counter the negative publicity that emanates almost daily from western media outlets. That means plunging headlong into the propaganda business, however repugnant it may seem.

Drastic step

An equally drastic solution would be for Ottawa to muscle in on provincial jurisdictions and provide large sums of money for the teaching of French. It could also encourage massive student exchange programs and try to persuade westerners to travel "out east" — even bribing them to go if necessary with special tax concessions for expenditures incurred in Quebec.

The cost would be enormous but it would be negligible compared with the cost of trying to run this country without Quebec.

If nothing is done about the tensions in this country and if the angry mood of the West continues unchecked, then Quebeckers will feel justified to react to the bitterness around them and opt for separatism in desperation.

Questions

1. Debate the substance of the letter to the editor of *Quest* magazine.

2. Attempt a response to Chaput-Rolland's question, "Why hang on to Confederation...?" Exchange viewpoints with a classmate. Evaluate the extent to which your classmate's response is convincing.

3. To what extent is Canada based on the types of compromises identified by J. Deutsch?

4. The author of "There's Still Hope for This Country" argues that "there is still hope... if people can somehow communicate." What measures does he propose to achieve communication? Do you feel such measures would be effective? What additional measures would you propose?

2
Why Is Language at the Heart of French-English Relations?

The role of language is to draw together all those who share traditions, customs, and sentiments. It is the primary medium by which a culture and nation are shaped, the medium through which one's relationship with the community is established. Language is the symbol of a national culture. To be deprived of one's language is to be deprived on one's national personality and collective identity.

Since the Conquest of New France in 1759, the status of the French language in Canada has been a subject of fierce dispute between anglophones and francophones. This was true when this land was a group of North American colonies in the British Empire and remained true later when Canada became a predominantly English-speaking federal state. For French Canadians — one of the two founding peoples — language has been even more than simply a medium of communication, important as that is to every human being; it has been and remains a question of the survival of their culture, their collective identity.

In the 1960s many Canadians expressed concern with the tensions existing between French and English and with the tendency of French Canadians in Quebec to reject Confederation as it had evolved. In 1963, in response to this anxiety, the federal government appointed a Royal Commission on Bilingualism and Biculturalism.

In its Preliminary Report (1965), the Commissioners wrote that "... Canada, without being fully conscious of the fact, was passing through the greatest crisis in its history." (p.13)

Since the 1960s new issues have been added to the seemingly endless list of disputes over language rights. We hear, for example, that a large public employees union, the Public Service Alliance of Canada, may advise its members to stop being bilingual and speak only French (the mother tongue of most people holding bilingual positions) if the issue of wage bonuses for bilingual jobs is not satisfactorily settled. In Vancouver debate rages over a proposed French television station; while in Windsor, high school students demand their promised French-language high school. In Toronto in September 1976 a large number of fans attending a Canada Cup hockey game booed the public announcements made in French. René Lévesque, premier of Quebec and leader of the separatist Parti Québécois, said at the time that this incident demonstrated that Canada's French and English are no longer "two solitudes ... but two hostilities."

After the Quebec election of November 1976 most Canadians began to give serious consideration to the state of relations between French- and English-speaking peoples. Although the election of the Parti Québécois was not necessarily a vote for separation from the rest of Canada, the Quebec government announced its intention to hold a referendum to decide this crucial matter in late 1979 or 1980.

Whether Quebeckers decide for or against becoming a "sovereign" state in "association" with Canada, the Quebec government will be implementing numerous measures to protect and develop the Québécois culture and the French language. To understand this important aspect of contemporary history it is necessary to consider why linguistic and cultural preservation are so important to Quebeckers.

Questions

1. "The Conquest" of 1759 appears important to an understanding of French–English relations. To what extent do the following "legal frameworks" provide evidence of hostility or mistrust or harmony between the two linguistic groups?
    Articles of Capitulation, 1759
    Proclamation Act, 1763
    Quebec Act, 1774
    Constitutional Act, 1791

2. Define "referendum." Give reasons why referendums are not used regularly.

QUEBEC'S CULTURAL SURVIVAL

Through the years, incident after incident has created a relationship between French- and English-speaking Canadians filled with suspicion and tension.

Because the Canadian colonies were part of the British Empire, influential English-speaking people in British North America felt that the national language should be English. Perhaps the clearest expressions of this sentiment came in the Durham Report of 1839 — a report on the affairs of British North America.

As a result of the rebellions of 1837 and 1838, Durham was appointed governor of the Canadas. In his report to the crown he stressed the need for assimilation of the French-Canadian culture of Lower Canada as the only suitable policy to follow. Durham proposed that "the first object ought to be that of making it [Lower Canada] an English province." Durham's proposal to assimilate the French Canadians was adopted in the Act of Union of 1840, but later abandoned; however, his basic attitude has been perpetuated by some groups of English-speaking Canadians up to the present day.

EXTRACTS FROM DURHAM'S REPORT

... if the British government intends to maintain its hold of the Canadas, it can rely on the English population alone.... The French Canadians ... are but the remains of an ancient colonization, and are and must be isolated in the midst of an Anglo-Saxon world....

There can hardly be conceived a nationality more destitute of all that can invigorate and elevate a people, than that which is exhibited by the descendants of the French in Lower Canada, owing to their retention of a peculiar language and manners. They are a people with no history, and no literature....

I entertain no doubts as to the national character which must be given to Lower Canada: it must be that of the British Empire ... it must henceforth be the first and steady purposes of the British Government to establish an English population with English laws and language in this province and to trust its government to none but a decidedly English Legislature.... The English have ... the decided superiority of intelligence on their side.... It will be an advantage to the French Canadians to acquire an English character.... The first object ought to be that of making it an English province and that with this end in view, the ascendancy should never again be placed in any hands but those of an English population. Lower Canada must be governed now, as it must be hereafter, by an English population.

– J. H. Stewart Reid et al., *A Source Book of Canadian History: Selected Documents and Personal Papers* (Toronto: Longmans Canada, 1959, revised ed., 1964), pp.111–12

Forty years later, Goldwin Smith was to echo a similar sentiment:

French Canada is a relic of the historical past preserved by isolation, as Siberian mammoths are preserved in ice.

– Goldwin Smith, *The Political Destiny of Canada* (1878), quoted in John Robert Colombo, *Colombo's Canadian Quotations* (Edmonton: Hurtig, 1974), p.552

In spite of the initial adoption of the Durham Report's recommendation that English should be the sole official language of Canada, the resistance of French Canadians to this stipulation gradually made French a working language in the legislature which represented both Upper and Lower Canada. When John A. Macdonald, George-Etienne Cartier, and others sought to find a basis for a confederation of all British colonies in North America, they accepted the French fact as an integral reality of the new union, as reflected in the British North America Act.

The 1867 BNA Act, which united the two Canadas, New Brunswick, and Nova Scotia into a federal state, contained some guarantees for the preservation of the French language.

This Act recognized English and French as Canada's two main languages. Both the English and French languages were given specific linguistic rights in section 133 of this constitution:

Either the English or the French language may be used by any person in the Debates of the House of the Parliament of Canada and of the House of the Legislature of Quebec; and both those Languages shall be used in the respective Records and Journals of those Houses; and either of those Languages may be used by any person or any Pleading or Process in or issuing from any Court of Canada established under this Act....

– *BNA Act, 1867*

Although the foundation for the equality of French and English in Quebec and in some federal institutions was established at the time of Confederation, the extent and limits of these language rights have been in dispute since 1867. In spite of this debate, however, and even after recognizing the contribution made by other ethnic groups to the building of Canada, most Canadians have acknowledged that English and French are the enduring languages of the two peoples who have formed this country.

Questions
1. Speculate as to the response a French Canadian would have had to Lord Durham's Report at the time of its appearance.

2. "French Canada is a relic of the historical past preserved by isolation. . . ." Do you think that Goldwin Smith's remark has any validity to today's situation?

THE "QUIET REVOLUTION" IN QUEBEC

Since the late 1950s a new technologically sophisticated Québécois nationalism has developed into a strong force in Quebec. An important landmark in the new nationalism was the coming to power in June 1960 of the Liberal party led by Jean Lesage. This new government, which replaced the twenty-year regime of Maurice Duplessis, promised Quebeckers that they would become "Maîtres Chez Nous" — Masters in Our Own House. The next six years of reform is commonly termed Quebec's *Quiet Revolution*.

The Quiet Revolution reflected the urbanization of the province during the previous fifty years. Quebec, like Ontario, had become a predominantly urban society and needed institutions and legislation to reflect this new reality.

The Quiet Revolution ushered in several long-awaited major reforms. Economically, the most important change was the nationalization of Quebec Hydro in 1962 — some fifty-seven years after Ontario had established public ownership in the electrical energy field. Quebec Hydro, as one of the largest corporations in the province, was to be operated mainly by French-Canadian engineers and administrators. This was something new for Quebec, where English-Canadian and American personnel had usually filled top offices in commerce and industry. Quebec Hydro and its logo "Q" became a symbol of the ability of francophone Quebeckers to be "Maîtres Chez Nous." René Lévesque, then a senior cabinet minister in the Liberal Lesage government, had been the prime catalyst in the move to put control and ownership of electrical energy in the hands of Quebec and its people.

One of the institutions which reflected the new climate in the province was the trade union movement. Until the late 1940s Quebec had both a Catholic-based and a secular union movement. By the late 1950s the trade union movement had been transformed from the most conservative and cautious in Canada into the most militant and socially minded in the country, with an increasingly nationalist tone. The trade union movement had three major components: the Confederation of National Trade Unions (a product of the original Catholic Unions), the Quebec Federation of Labour (connecting both International, that is, US-based, and Canadian unions), and various groups of teachers. These three groups were to cooperate in the formation of a common front and in the general strikes organized jointly in the 1970s.

Another major change brought by the Quiet Revolution was the complete overhauling of the educational system. In 1964 Quebec established its first-ever ministry of education, with responsibility for the whole provincial system. What had previously been mainly a religious-oriented system, with staff primarily recruited from the teaching orders of the Catholic church, now became a public, secular system offering a much-revised curriculum which mirrored the social and technological changes characteristic of the Quiet Revolution. Between 1960 and 1965 Quebec experienced the most rapid expansion of any educational system in Canada.

Tens of thousands of students enrolled in new postsecondary institutions, which emphasized technological, commercial, and cultural studies. Just as the labor force allied itself with movements for collective survival so too did students express a heightened nationalism. In 1968, ten thousand French-Canadian students demonstrated for a new French-language university and more jobs. One year later they demanded that McGill

University — closely associated with the English community — be turned into a French institution.

The Quiet Revolution also saw a vast expansion of Quebec's cultural life. Singers, actors and actresses, dancers, writers and producers, TV and radio performers and personalities, theatres, movies, and touring companies, vast sales of popular records, books, and magazines — all burst upon the Quebec scene. A new Quebec francophone culture asserted itself and created among Quebeckers a self-confidence and national self-definition which was the envy of their English-Canadian compatriots. In addition, Quebec introduced a series of social reforms and programs which included improvements in public health services and pensions.

However, these changes and reforms did not appear to meet the economic aspirations of Quebeckers. The Commission on Bilingualism and Biculturalism released statistics which demonstrated the disadvantaged position of francophones both in English Canada and in Quebec.

Table 1 / Average Labor Income of Male Salary- and Wage-Earners by Ethnic Origin – Quebec, 1961

	Labor Income	
	Dollars	Index
General average	*3469*	*100.0*
Ethnic Origin		
British	4940	142.4
Scandinavians	4939	142.4
Dutch	4891	140.9
Jewish	4851	139.8
Russians	4828	139.1
Germans	4254	122.6
Poles	3984	114.8
Asians	3734	107.6
Ukrainians	3733	107.6
Other Europeans	3547	102.4
Hungarians	3537	101.9
French	3185	91.8
Italians	2938	84.6
Native Indians	2112	60.8

Source: *Report of the Royal Commission on Bilingualism and Biculturalism,* Book III: The Work World (Ottawa: Queen's Printer, 1969), p.23.

Francophone Quebeckers became increasingly conscious of the necessity to assert themselves politically. In 1966 the Union Nationale was returned to power on a "Québec d'abord" (Quebec first) platform, and an independence party, the Rassemblement pour l'Indépendance Nationale, received 9 percent of the vote. This was the first time that such a significant "indépendantiste" sentiment had expressed itself at the polls.

At the end of the 1970s the tension between French and English Canadians had become clearly defined. The election in November 1976 by Quebeckers of a government dedicated to an independent Quebec, in a new association with the rest of Canada, would obviously have far-reaching effects for this country. Understanding *why* Quebeckers see themselves as a national collectivity or nation is essential to understanding how the possibility of Quebec sovereignty has arisen.

Questions
1. For what reasons have the changes in Quebec during the '60s been described as revolutionary?
2. Reflect on the phrase "Maîtres Chez Nous." What powers must a people possess if they are truly to be masters in their own house?
3. Examine the table on page 24. What reasons might explain the low average income of French Canadians relative to other ethnic groups?

THE IMPORTANCE OF LANGUAGE TO CULTURAL SURVIVAL

In June 1975, at a St. Jean Baptiste celebration, tens of thousands of francophones stood on top of Mount Royal in Montreal, and took an oath not to speak English for a year. To understand this event, we must examine the role of the French language in French-Canadian culture.

As we have seen, the use of one's language is not an isolated social phenomenon, it is at the heart of cultural survival; language and culture are inseparably linked. Language is the most evident expression of culture, and, in turn, a cultural identity revolves around and is maintained by a shared language. Language expresses the way people think; it expresses the particular way they feel and describes the world as they perceive it.

> Culture is a way of *being, thinking and feeling*. It is a driving force animating a significant group of individuals united by a common tongue and sharing the *same customs, habits and experiences*. [italics added]
>
> – *Report of the Royal Commission on Bilingualism and Biculturalism*, Book I: The Official Languages (Ottawa: Queen's Printer, 1967), p.xxxi

In *An Option for Quebec* (1968), René Lévesque described the meshing of language and culture when he explained what it means to be Québécois. He said that the Québécois are a people emotionally attached to a place — Quebec — where they feel at home. In this "homeland," French-Canadian culture has developed for three and a half centuries. Lévesque argued that the protection of language is necessary to the continued development of the "Québécois personality."

At the core of this personality is the fact that we speak French. Everything else depends on this one essential element and follows from it or leads us infallibly back to it. (p.19)

The Commission on Bilingualism and Biculturalism also emphasized the relationship between language and culture when it described language as the "key" to cultural development and "a necessary condition for the complete preservation of a culture." The very name of this influential commission linked language and culture.

Language, however, does not exist in a vacuum. Even in Quebec the survival of the French language is jeopardized by the impact of a number of forces. One of the major threats is the fact that French-speaking people are greatly outnumbered by English-speaking people in North America. Constant exposure to English through magazines, radio, and television has resulted in a decreasing use of French, and this trend will continue unless counteractive measures are taken.

Economic factors can also influence what language will dominate. For example, because most large corporations use English to do business, many French Canadians have found that unless they learn English, many job opportunities will be denied them. Even in Quebec, where the majority of people speak French, it has been commonly assumed that English is the language of commerce and opportunity. (This is usually the reason given by immigrants for wanting their children to be educated in English.) Indeed, there are some who believe that this trend in the use of English is irreversible given the fact that the upper managerial ranks are integrated into the multinational corporations.

Thus it is no accident that all of Quebec's governments since the late 1960s have been concerned with the issue of language. All three of Quebec's major parties — the Union Nationale, the Liberal Party, and the Parti Québécois — have passed legislation to protect and strengthen the role of French in the province's economic, cultural, and political life.

In spite of important political and philosophical differences among them, all parties in Quebec have responded to the needs and desires of francophone Quebeckers to establish French as the dominant and enduring language of their province.

The most recent legislation on the French language has been embodied in Quebec's Official Language Charter — Bill 101 — passed in 1977. The Language Charter, as well as the federal government's Official Languages Act (1969), has been the subject of much debate in Quebec and across Canada.

From the discussion of these two pieces of legislation in chapter 4, you will notice once again that the debate revolves essentially around the theme of collective versus individual rights and the extent to which these can be combined.

PERSPECTIVES: LANGUAGE AND FRENCH–ENGLISH RELATIONS

The following excerpts illustrate various aspects of the language issue in the context of French–English relations. The excerpts from Sellar's and Siegfried's books are printed as examples of the longevity of the language issue question in the history of this country. The excerpt from the Task Force on Canadian Unity is included as a particularly illuminating description of the uniqueness of Quebec.

* * *

In order to be psychologically well, and in order to be fully creative, I think people need a strong political identity, a sense of territory. I don't even think it's a question that can be debated, it's a biological imperative. Quebec would not appear so disruptive to the, shall

I say, order of Canada, if the rest of Canada were equally strong and concerned with its future.

     – Geneviève Bujold, quoted in John Hofsess, "Emergence of Claude Jutra," in *Maclean's Magazine*, August 1973, p.71

. . . I was in Quebec City recently, a marvelous, wonderful place. I saw some models of French sculpture, but my motel was as American as you can imagine; the food was completely American. The only difference was the language, for Lord's sake, plus a few intellectuals who make poetry and stuff. Hell, that's not French culture. They're as far away from France as the rest of the Canadians are from England. I mean, how in hell can they be independent? It's all nonsense.

     – Gunnar Myrdal, Swedish social scientist, quoted by Peter C. Newman in *Home Country: People, Places, and Power Politics* (Toronto: McClelland and Stewart, 1973), p.51

FRENCH NATIONALISTS — A "NUISANCE" IN PARLIAMENT

Nationalism has produced a type of Canadian unknown thirty years ago, who shouts French when he knows he who asks him a question speaks only English, telephones in French, demands what he wants in French, persists in using his mother-tongue as an instrument to humiliate his English neighbor. Then there is a new air of superiority to make the English feel they are unwelcome intruders. When a Canadian of this sort is elected a representative he makes himself a nuisance in parliament. He lies in wait for fancied slights and omissions, yelling "En Français," demands "une sou" be stamped on coppers, and French words on postage stamps; is loud in denouncing appointments in English to office and asking that more salary be paid some official in his country.

     – Robert Sellar, *The Tragedy of Quebec: The Expulsion of Its Protestant Farmers* (1907; reprinted ed., Toronto: University of Toronto Press, 1974), p.285

A NOT VERY PLEASANT OBSTINACY

What Frenchman of France has not been shocked to see in cities so French in their population as Montreal or Quebec a form of civilization other than his own dominating openly, uncontested? Quebec, for instance, does not give the immediate impression of a city of ours; many sensitively observant visitors have felt that. In this city of 68,000, of whom not more than 10,000 are English, there are many parts where French is not understood: perhaps it would be more accurate to say where people will not understand it. On the railways it is tolerated at best. At the Chateau Frontenac Hotel, that marvel of comfort and elegance created by the Canadian Pacific, the principal employees do perhaps understand it, but they refuse to speak it. It is true that in the inquiry office and in the kitchen you can hear it spoken as much as you like, but is it not pitiful that English should be the speech of the managers, and French of the menials? The French Canadians have come to put up with this kind of not very pleasant obstinacy. They learn English, and in that they are wise enough; but they have never been able to get their rivals to learn

French. And therein we cannot but recognize a really significant defeat.

It is the same in Montreal. Visitors may pass whole weeks there, frequenting hotels, banks, shops, railway stations, without ever imagining for a moment that the town is French by a great majority of its inhabitants. English society affects unconsciousness of this fact, and bears itself exactly as though it had no French neighbours. They seem to regard Montreal as their property. As they have got to this height, not by force of votes or of numbers, it must be admitted that their attitude is the outcome of the old sense of the rights of the conqueror. Think of the Indian civil service, and you will understand better the rulers of Canada.

– André Siegfried, The Race Question in Canada (1906; reprinted ed., Toronto: McClelland and Stewart, 1966), p. 185

It is simply because, as every French Canadian who is sensitive fully knows, the English Canadian thinks himself instinctively superior to people of French descent. Even the more open-minded English Canadian cannot accept the idea of two nations in Canada, and he will never tolerate political duality. He cannot conceive that fourteen million people can be equal to four million, and because he is three times stronger he naturally thinks himself three times superior. Even if by some unexpected miracle the B.N.A. Act could be amended so that French Canadians living outside Quebec would become equal to English Canadians, most historians, politicians, experts, intellectuals would never share with Quebec in the great decisions of Canada.

– Solange Chaput-Rolland, My Country: Canada or Quebec? (Toronto: Macmillan, 1966), pp. 111–12.

QUEBEC: A DISTINCT SOCIETY

One can readily identify several factors which have led to the emergence of a distinct society in modern Quebec. We have identified six: history, language, law, common origins, feelings and politics — which, together with others, have led to the development of a distinct society in modern Quebec.

The first, then, is history — the legacy of over three hundred years of the continuous development of a people. During much of this period, but particularly after Confederation, it was possible to speak of a single French-Canadian community which extended to many parts of what is now Canada and to which Quebec contributed a substantial portion of the leadership and the vision to sustain it. French Canada, like English Canada, was knit together from distinct regional societies which, over time, came to think of themselves, for at least some purposes, as one. However, the changes in Canadian social structure since the Second World War have drastically weakened the organic links between these communities. What now is emerging from the old French Canada is a strong and vital Quebec, and many more vulnerable smaller and weaker French-Canadian communities in other provinces, each of which has been forced by circumstances and a constant threat of assimilation to set its own course independently of, and sometimes in opposition to, developments within Quebec. This process, rooted in the history of Canada generally, would by itself designate Quebec as the most viable and important locus of the French culture in North America; yet there are other, equally important, factors.

The second important factor is language. Quebec is home to over 85 per cent of all citizens who speak French, and 81 per cent of Quebec's population is French-speaking. Current demographic data for Canada as a whole reveal a growing linguistic territorial concentration which is rendering Quebec increasingly French and the rest of the country, excluding New Brunswick, increasingly English.

A third factor is Canada's legal duality. Quebec was authorized by the Quebec Act of 1774 to retain its French civil laws. One year before Confederation, the civil laws were codified along the lines of the *Code Napoléon*. Amended from time to time since then, the civil code is the basis of Quebec's private law while the other provinces have lived under the English common law tradition, thus producing two distinct legal systems.

A fourth factor contributing to Quebec's unique character is the distinctive ethnic group or people which French Canadians form. The majority of these are persons whose families came to North America several centuries ago. While the more recent arrivals from France have been somewhat less likely to settle in Quebec, a majority still does so. This means that in addition to the linguistic distinctiveness of the province may be added the fact that the ethnic origins of its majority are shared. Quebec is simply not a multicultural society in the same sense as many other parts of Canada. Although it has become more ethnically diverse in the last few decades, particularly in the Montreal area, Quebec is and will remain predominantly French in language and in ethnicity; it is unique in Canada on both of these counts.

There remain two other factors which must be added. The legacy of history, a shared language and common origins are all important social facts in their own right, but they say nothing about the feelings of Québécois, a fifth factor which marks Quebec off from the other provinces. The shared desires, aspirations and even the fears of the collectivity provide perhaps the most compelling evidence in support of Quebec's cultural distinctiveness.

For the longest part of Quebec's history one theme dominated the cultural life of the collectivity. That theme was *survivance,* or sheer survival. This overriding concern for the maintenance of the way of life of a people coloured the relationship between Quebecers and their compatriots, and it continues to do so. Yet only an insensitive observer of the life of the province could fail to note a substantial shift in approach in which that collectivity's concern for survival is now expressed by the thoroughly contemporary and dynamic pursuit of its own development, or what has been often described as *épanouissement* (literally, "blooming," "blossoming").

Psychologically, the transition from *survivance* to *épanouissement* has been accompanied by a remarkable alteration in Quebecers' attitudes toward themselves. This may be described as the shift in self-perception of French-speaking Quebecers from a Canadian minority only grudgingly accepted in many parts of Canada to a Québécois majority increasingly confident and determined to secure its future.

This transformation is reflected in the very vocabulary that Quebecers have used to describe themselves. Orginally, the French-speaking people of Quebec called themselves *Canadiens* and referred to the English-speaking people as *les Anglais*. In the middle and late nineteenth century, they began calling themselves *Canadiens français* to distinguish themselves from English-speaking Canadians. In recent years, however, more and more have adopted the name and identity of *Québécois*, underlining this sense of themselves as a majority, as a people.

Parallel to this development, French Canadians elsewhere in Canada increasingly have come to see themselves as a part of their provincial communities rather than as members of a comprehensive French Canadian society. They describe themselves as *Franco-Ontariens, Franco-Manitobains, Fransaskois,* and collectively as *les francophones hors Québec* outside of Quebec.

These changes suggest the sixth and final factor contributing to the distinctiveness of the province of Quebec — namely, the changing meaning of politics to a society in transition. The psychological passage from minority to majority has been marked by the wholesale appropriation of the state for this cultural struggle. The last several decades have produced leaders in Quebec, as elsewhere, who are prepared to employ the resources of the provincial state to achieve collective goals and to promote rapid social and economic development.

History, language, law, ethnicity, feelings and politics render Quebec at once a society, a province and the stronghold of the French-Canadian people. Taken together, these factors produce in the Québécois a vision of Quebec as the living heart of the French presence in North America; collectively they are as strong or as weak as Quebec is: no more, no less. It is this reality with which other Canadians and the Canadian federal system must come to terms. For the people of Quebec, the question that remains to be answered is whether they can better serve their future within Canada and its federal system or whether they would do better standing on their own.

– The Task Force on Canadian Unity, *A Future Together: Observations and Recommendations* (Ottawa: January 1979), pp. 23–25

Questions

1. To what extent do you identify with a particular culture? What are the special characteristics of it? To what degree is the culture with which you identify "a way of being, thinking and feeling"?

2. What reasons are given to explain the domination of one language over another? Assess the impact of these factors on Canada's relationship with the United States.

3. Summarize one of the excerpts in the section "Perspectives: Language and French-English Relations" and suggest the significance of it to the contemporary debate.

4. The Task Force on Canadian Unity lists six factors which have led to the formation of modern Quebec. To what extent are these factors also characteristic of English Canada?

3
Bilingualism in the Control Tower: The Air Traffic Control Dispute of 1976

BACKGROUND

This chapter concentrates on a major controversy that revealed serious tension between French and English Canadians over the language question. Whether French was to be used, along with English, in the control towers of Quebec's airports was the main issue of dispute in the strike of air pilots in the summer of 1976. Many people were worried that the disruption of air traffic might continue for months and jeopardize the success of the Olympic Games being held that year in Montreal.

The remarkable thing about the strike was how quickly people in the entire country took one side or the other. Generally, English Canadians took the stand that *air safety* was at the heart of the conflict and that French should not be used in directing air traffic over Quebec. They agreed with the English-speaking pilots and controllers who maintained that bilingual (that is, English and French) ground-air communication was not as safe as unilingual communication (that is, English only).

French-speaking Quebeckers felt *safety* was not a valid argument against bilingualism in air communications. Bilingual air control had been working safely for years in many airports around the world. They felt the issue was basically one of their right as Canadian citizens to work in their mother tongue, especially in Quebec.

In the summer of '76 this dispute had developed into what some observers then called "the worst crisis since conscription." That was before the election of the Parti Québécois as the government of Quebec in November 1976.

The heated debate over the language of air control was largely the result of a two-century-old tension between the French and the English. Acceptance or rejection of French as one of two official languages in Canada is an issue that had arisen many times; this air strike brought the tension into the open once more.

> The fact that this particular application of bilingualism (re: control tower) has turned into a vehicle for every nut and bigot in the country to vent his spleen on — one set of T shirts showing a beaver in helmet and goggles, strangling a frog; another set saying, "where are you General Wolfe, now that we need you?" — makes me sick to my stomach. But the thought of dying in a mid-air collision over Dorval makes me even sicker.
>
> – Sandra Gwyn, "The Surly Bonds of Bigotry,"
> *Saturday Night*, April 1977, p. 15

Although it is important to understand the facts of the air traffic control dispute, it is essential to see it against the historical background which produced this particular conflict.

THE AIR TRAFFIC CONTROL DISPUTE

On July 1, 1976, while Canada celebrated its 109th birthday as a country, many Canadians were worried that this might be one of the last Dominion Days with Confederation intact. The country seemed to be splitting apart at the seams. A nine-day strike by Canadian pilots had brought air travel to a standstill. With the Olympics looming in the near future and no compromise in sight, the government appeared helpless.

The pilots' association said they would not fly until it was agreed that English was to be the only language used for control at Montreal's international airports — Dorval and Mirabel. Bilingual air traffic control had been opposed by both English-speaking controllers and pilots since the program began in smaller Quebec airports, which used only visual controls. They maintained that even though bilingualism was working in several European countries, unilingual control was safer. Their position was firm and, as mentioned earlier, the vast majority of English-speaking Canadians supported their stand.

The French-speaking pilots and controllers held the opposite view. They argued that it was safer to have French as the language of communication between French-speaking pilots and controllers. This was the principle on which the United Nations's International Civil Aviation Organization (ICAO) had based its policy. The ICAO allows two choices: the local language normally used in ground communication and the universal language (English). Applied to Quebec, where 80 percent of the population is francophone, this would mean that the normal language of ground communication over Quebec airports would be French, while English-speaking pilots could use English to land.

Two languages — the national language and English — are used at many airports in the western world, including Paris, Rome, Lisbon, Madrid, and Athens, where Air Canada and CP Air pilots land regularly. Yet English-speaking pilots felt that a similar system would be unworkable in Quebec.

To end the strike, the Minister of Transport, Otto Lang, negotiated a truce whereby an inquiry commission of three judges would be set up to investigate and decide whether bilingualism should exist in all Quebec air communications. To reach this agreement the government made several major concessions to the representatives of the predominantly antibilingual Canadian Air Line Pilots Association (CALPA) and the Canadian Air Traffic Control Association (CATCA).

The original proposal was for a two-man inquiry but this was expanded to three — the third member to be approved by the predominantly English-speaking airmen. The controllers also gained a say in the selection of the technical advisors that could work with the commission, while CALPA was given the right to submit a minority report with the commission's findings. The final concession was equally unacceptable to the francophones involved in the dispute. The agreement put the entire onus of evidence on the probilingual supporters. They had to demonstrate that bilingualism was safer than, or as safe as, unilingualism and answer any objections raised by CATCA or CALPA.

Most English-speaking Canadians were pleased with the compromise. The reaction among francophones, on the other hand, was overwhelmingly negative. They said that it contradicted the federal bilingual policy.

The Globe and Mail, *Toronto*,
July 1, 1976

Marchand Quits Over Air Bilingualism

By William Johnson
Globe and Mail Reporter

OTTAWA — Environment Minister Jean Marchand quit the Cabinet yesterday in anger over the agreement signed by Transport Minister Otto Lang with English-speaking pilots and traffic controllers.

The move came as Government members worked to heal a split among federal Liberals over the issue, seeking a way to meet the demands of Quebec MPs, pilots and controllers without losing Mr. Lang, who was reported ready to resign if the agreement is altered.

Prime Minister Pierre Trudeau, emerging from a four-hour Liberal caucus meeting last night, confirmed that he had accepted the resignation, but refused to comment further.

Mr. Marchand, who will continue as a backbench MP, would say to reporters only that his decision is final and that "I'm going home. I've been a minister for 11 years so I can relax for a couple of months, no?"

Solicitor-General Warren Allmand, one of the few Liberals who would comment, said he was "astounded" by the resignation. Mr. Marchand's action came suddenly and unexpectedly, with even close colleagues unaware of it until it became general knowledge.

Earlier, Mr. Allmand had dismissed the rumors of the resignation as "ridiculous."

Mr. Marchand's letter of resignation, released last night by the Prime Minister's Office, refers to serious "mistakes," "faults" and "gaps" in the agreement signed Monday by Mr. Lang.

"It would be impossible for me under the circumstances to abide by the rules of ministerial solidarity," Mr. Marchand said, indicating he wants to speak out against the agreement. He promises an "exhaustive analysis" of it at the first opportunity.

The former minister was bitter toward Progressive Conservative Leader Joseph Clark and NDP Leader Edward Broadbent. The problem could have been solved "if the Opposition had acted responsibly." Mr. Clark "played petty, small-minded politics" instead of considering "the common good of this country."

He said it was impossible to change some of the objectionable parts of the agreement without "bringing back chaos to air transport in Canada."

Mr. Trudeau said yesterday in the Commons that the agreement negotiated with the unions could not now be changed without destroying the peace that had been negotiated.

A wave of bitterness swept the Liberals when the terms of the agreement negotiated by Mr. Lang with air traffic controllers and pilots to end a week-long national air tieup were made public on Monday.

Mr. Lang talked late Monday with Treasury Board President Jean Chretien, Health Minister Marc Lalonde, Liberal MPs Serge Joyal and Pierre De Bane, and representatives of l'Association des Gens de l'Air, who represent the French-Canadian pilots and air traffic controllers from Quebec at odds with their own unions.

The French aviation people, backed by Mr. Joyal, Mr. De Bane and, according to reports, by Mr. Marchand, presented demands that the Government now is trying to meet without destroying the agreement that sent English-speaking pilots back to work.

The demands have been kept confidential, as Government representatives and the French airmen feared a backlash by English-speaking controllers and pilots.

It was Mr. Marchand, when he was transport minister in June, 1974, who first instituted bilingualism at five small Quebec airports. He was immediately opposed by pilots and air traffic controllers from all other parts of the country who set out to defeat the bilingualism policy.

The Globe and Mail, *Toronto,*
October 14, 1976

Language Proposals for Constitution Cited by Richardson in His Resignation

By Hugh Winsor
Globe and Mail Reporter

OTTAWA — Defence Minister James Richardson resigned from the Cabinet yesterday in opposition to proposals for patriating the Canadian constitution that would lock in French language and cultural guarantees.

Mr. Richardson, 54-year-old member of the wealthy Winnipeg business family, told a press conference he resigned from the Government to "obtain freedom to speak openly and publicly without the constraints imposed by my position in the Cabinet."

Well known for his insistence in Cabinet that more be done by government for Western Canada, Mr. Richardson has also made known his unhappiness about the Government's bilingualism policies, which are particularly unpopular in the West.

While his career as a Cabinet minister has often been lacklustre, his resignation on this issue comes at a particularly bad time for Prime Minister Pierre Trudeau and his Government.

Mr. Trudeau said he regretted Mr. Richardson's resignation as "premature." The Cabinet, he said, had made no decision on patriating the constitution in a form that would entrench French and English in the federal Government service.

Mr. Trudeau's popularity has already been severely hurt in English Canada by the bilingualism backlash and Mr. Richardson's resignation, regardless of the merits of his arguments on the constitution, will be another festering point for anti-French sentiment.

The gist of Mr. Richardson's argument is that the constitutional guarantees for French combined with an amending formula that would give Quebec a permanent veto over constitutional changes will commit Canadians in the future to a linguistic straitjacket.

Mr. Richardson said the bilingualism policy is not working and that it is premature "for a country which is still feeling its way" to adopt a permanent position until it can be shown that bilingualism will work.

Denying suggestions that his resignation will exacerbate tension over the language issue, Mr. Richardson said the policy has already been divisive and he felt he should speak out before irrevocable steps are taken.

Also, two studies of bilingual air traffic control had already been done — the Lisson study of 1969 and a further study in 1971; both had recommended bilingual air communication.

In Ottawa, Environment Minister Jean Marchand, former Minister of Transport, resigned his post in Prime Minister Trudeau's cabinet over the signing of the agreement, which he felt was filled with serious "mistakes and gaps."

Communications Minister Jeanne Sauvé, also a member of the Trudeau cabinet, described the agreement that ended the strike as "kneeling down to a bunch of fanatics." The National Assembly of Quebec, in a rare unanimous vote, supported the position of the Quebec pilots and controllers. The Quebec government also offered financial assistance if the provincial section of CATCA incurred expenses in their campaign to expand bilingual air control. Three months later, Defence Minister James Richardson resigned because recognition of French had, in his opinion, gone too far in the Liberal government.

The outpouring of anti-French feeling in English Canada during the dispute was perhaps a major factor in the increased support given the PQ. The proportion of the popular vote rose from 30 percent in 1973 to 41 percent in 1976 thereby ensuring the Parti Québécois a strong majority in Quebec's National Assembly after the election of November 15. A month later

Lévesque got his pilot to call Dorval in French — "Nobody can tell the pilot of a Quebec Government plane not to speak French over Quebec" *(The Globe and Mail,* Toronto, December 15, 1976).

At the heart of the debate over bilingual air control was the question of French Canada's place in Confederation. For many Quebeckers the matter in dispute was one of collective right. Denial of the right to use their language in daily work was perceived as a serious threat to the cultural survival of the French Canadian. As one federal MP commented:

> Even the most moderate French Canadian will rise up when the use of French in Quebec is threatened.
>
> – John Ciaccia (Liberal MP, Lower Mount Royal), quoted in Richard Cleroux, "Quebec Outrage Builds Against Air Agreement," *The Globe and Mail*, Toronto, July 3, 1976

Prime Minister Trudeau called the dispute the most serious crisis since the Conscription Crisis of the Second World War: "The issue in this regard is indeed national unity and no other issue." The Task Force on Canadian Unity, presenting reasons why English and French Canada were drifting apart, declared:

> The reaction of English-speaking Canada to the air traffic controllers' strike (known in French as the *Gens de l'air* affair) during the spring and summer of 1976 played an important symbolic role in convincing some Québécois of the lack of understanding to be looked for from English-speaking Canada. For many Québécois, the vehemence with which the English-speaking controllers, pilots and public seemed to reject out of hand the right of French-speaking pilots and controllers to work in their own language, even in a province where they formed a substantial majority, was a clear revelation of the true state of French-English relations in Canada. In this way, the "bilingual backlash," of which the controllers' strike was perhaps the most dramatic example, clearly contributed to the Parti Québécois victory.
>
> – *A Future Together: Observations and Recommendations* (Ottawa: January, 1979), pp. 13–14

The possible separation of Quebec, which was thought to have been eliminated by the Official Languages Act, had surfaced again.

REACTIONS TO THE DISPUTE

An examination of the views of both English-speaking and French-speaking Canadians illustrates the serious implications of the sentiments expressed for·the development of national unity. The problem appears to be much deeper than the concern for safety. "Air safety" seems to have been a focus for unresolved tension between French and English Canadians.

The quotations in the following section have been chosen to illustrate the wide range of responses to the air traffic control dispute specifically, and bilingualism and French–English interaction generally. It is important to remember that these quotes are *illustrations* and that not all people in English or French Canada feel the same way.

The *first set of quotations* represents the unilingual English reaction to the air traffic control issue. As can be seen, antibilingual and anti-Quebec feelings are often mixed together. In many letters and telegrams sent to the government and newspapers, the air traffic dispute brought to the surface sentiments that appeared to have already been quite well developed.

A letter to the editor describes an often heard explanation for the hostile reactions on the part of many English-speaking Canadians.

> The main cause of the present dispute is a hatred by English for French Canadians, not very dissimilar to the situation in the southern U.S. a decade ago, or Rhodesia, South Africa and Northern Ireland today — the hatred of one group of people by another group because they are different, whether the difference be colour, religion or language. . . .
>
> *—The Globe and Mail,* Toronto, July 17, 1976

Although this explanation is something many Canadians do not like to discuss, the fact remains that there are varying degrees of prejudice between French- and English-speaking Canadians.

The negative reaction of francophone Canadians to the air traffic control settlement is illustrated by the *second set of quotations*. These were chosen because they are typical of the reactions of many Quebeckers. It is obvious that almost all francophone Quebeckers felt humiliated and angry by what they saw as an unjust compromise.

The letters and telegrams received by Transport Minister Otto Lang demonstrate that, on the whole, neither side of the dispute was communicating with the other:

> The letters are a dialogue of the deaf. The letters in English constitute almost without exception a long monologue against bilingualism. The letters in French, almost without exception, denounce the agreement signed by Mr. Lang and the striking unions.
>
> *– The Globe and Mail,* Toronto, July 10, 1976

This lack of communication between these two groups brings to mind the title of Hugh MacLennan's novel, *Two Solitudes*, which describes French–English relations in the early years of this century.

Such opposing views on the part of English and French Canadians have a long history and cannot be easily overcome. To understand the prospects for Canada's future as a unified or divided country, it is important to explore the *opinions* and *feelings* of these two groups in the air traffic control dispute. The most important question is not who was right about whether air traffic control should be bilingual in Quebec, but *why* the issue became such an explosive one. Why was there such poor communication between Canada's two founding groups after seven years of the official bilingualism policy, which had been supported by all major political parties in parliament?

ENGLISH CANADA'S REACTION

The depth of feeling aroused across English Canada by the dispute is revealed by the following comments from various parts of the country.

1. "As far as I'm concerned we should take a chain saw to Quebec and cut it off. Let it float right down the St. Lawrence." (Calgary, Alberta)
   The Globe and Mail, Toronto, July 5, 1976.

2. "I got the feeling people aren't going to wait for Quebec to separate. . . . they'll kick them out now.". . . In 1964, English Canada would have brought out the troops to keep Quebec in Confederation — but "now they'd make them

'My theory is, make Polish the first language of Canada and this French-English thing will disappear just like that.'

The Globe and Mail, Toronto, June 28, 1976

sandwiches and bid them bon voyage." (Max Saltsman, NDP member, Cambridge, Ontario) *The Globe and Mail*, Toronto, June 30, 1976.

3. "As the Westerners might say...'Let them freeze in the dark'...bilingually." (Ontario) *The Toronto Star*, July 3, 1976.

4. "We don't like having anything shoved down our throats, like they're trying to do with French...." (Annapolis Valley, Nova Scotia) *The Globe and Mail*, Toronto, July 5, 1976.

5. "One country, one language.... Let the majority rule." (British Columbia) *The Globe and Mail*, Toronto, July 5, 1976.

37

6. "There is a large German settlement here and many Chinese living in Vancouver. Why shouldn't these languages be officially recognized as there are more of these people here than there are French Canadians." (Fraser Valley, B.C.) *The Globe and Mail,* Toronto, July 5, 1976.

7. Bilingual control "is dangerous stuff." English is "the universal language" for air control but "here we are in Canada, just to appease Quebec, putting in French to control the traffic around Montreal airports." (Premier Frank Moores, St. John's, Newfoundland) *The Globe and Mail,* Toronto, June 26, 1976.

8. "I don't mind federal offices using English and French in Quebec but I get mad thinking of money spent so that someone on a holiday out West can buy stamps from a French-speaking clerk for postcards to send back to Quebec...." (British Columbia) *The Globe and Mail,* Toronto, July 6, 1976.

9. "Quebec and the French language are cancers which are destroying Canada. If, as Mr. Trudeau says, his style of bilingualism is necessary for the preservation of Confederation, then Confederation is not worth preserving. Let us cut out the cancer. Canada neither needs nor can afford Quebec...." (Calgary, Alberta) *The Globe and Mail,* Toronto, July 10, 1976.

10. "We have Italians, Polish, Dutch and German origins here — I do not hear them wanting to have their language forced on we, the English-speaking public. They keep their culture and language on a personal level and it works just fine. Canada is an English-speaking nation. If Quebec does not honour our language, let them return to France." (Highgate, Ontario) *The Globe and Mail,* Toronto, July 10, 1976.

FRENCH CANADA'S REACTION

French-Canadian reaction to the air traffic control dispute is illustrated in the following excerpts.

1. "You succeeded in getting the planes back in the air, but at what price? . . . I fear that the federal government dealt out of weakness to the outlaw pilots. Their blackmail was rewarded. But unity of Canada was, to the same extent, compromised." (Ottawa) *The Globe and Mail*, Toronto, July 10, 1976.

2. "One thing is sure – these events are causing the re-surfacing of a phenomenon that has been slightly forgotten since the last war, but never evaporated, English racism to Quebec." (Pierre Vadboneaur, Quebec writer and adviser to the Confederation of National Trade Unions) *The Toronto Star*, July, 3, 1976.

3. "I have always been pro-Canadian, . . . Now I owe it to myself to be entirely Québécois." (Ville d'Anjou, Montreal suburb, Quebec) *The Globe and Mail*, Toronto, July 10, 1976.

4. "English Canada is pushing Quebec out of Confederation." (Jean-Luc Patenaude, head of the Quebec Wing of CATCA) *The Toronto Sun*, June 29, 1976.

5. Letter to O. Lang: "You understand nothing. Your message [to French-speaking pilots and controllers] was betrayal and lies." (5 people from Rivière-du-Loup, Quebec) *The Globe and Mail*, Toronto, July 10, 1976.

'The pilot is fluent in English AND French. It's just one of those mornings he isn't speaking to ANYONE.'

6. "The Government has been blackmailed by English-speaking pilots and controllers guided by pure racism." (R. Demers, President of Association des Gens de l'Air) *The Globe and Mail*, Toronto, June 30, 1976.

7. "French in Quebec was mere justice. You are a bunch of frauds and cowards, you who are unable to be just towards French Canadians. 'Vive Quebec libre.' I think

that will be the slogan of French Canadians from now on." (Quebec) *The Globe and Mail*, Toronto, July 10, 1976.

8. ". . . the sad outcome of 109 years of federalism and eight years of French power." (René Lévesque, Leader of the Parti Québécois) *The Globe and Mail*, Toronto, June 30, 1976.

9. "This air bilingualism policy is a permissive policy to allow a French Canadian pilot in Quebec to be able to use his own language in Quebec without denying the right of any English pilot to use his language here. It's just incomprehensible to me how we could allow a group of pilots to divide the country like this."

– John Ciaccia, Liberal MP, Lower Mount Royal, quoted in Richard Cleroux, "Quebec Outrage Builds Against Air Agreement," *The Globe and Mail*, Toronto, July 3, 1976.

The Sault Star, *Sault Sainte Marie, Ontario, January 5, 1979*
Reprinted with permission of The Canadian Press

Bilingual Air Traffic Tests Prove Safe

OTTAWA (CP) – The federal transport department, after 18 months of testing, has concluded that a bilingual air traffic control system in Quebec "will have no detrimental impact on safety."

It goes further in saying that "some improvements in system safety may be achieved if the recommended procedures are implemented and rigorously applied."

The tests involved simulated air traffic over Dorval and Mirabel international airports. They were designed "to develop the necessary procedures in order to safely implement bilingual communications for aircraft under instrument flight rules in the province of Quebec."

The government decision in 1975 to expand bilingual air control services over Quebec brought work disruptions among air controllers and airline pilots in 1976 who wanted English-only used in air-ground communications.

There also was angry debate in the Commons over the issue, prompting Prime Minister Trudeau to say it posed the biggest threat to national unity since conscription was introduced in the Second World War.

The debate and the threatened work disruption led the government to appoint a three-member commission of inquiry into bilingual air traffic control. It is made up of Mr. Justice W.R. Sinclair of the Supreme Court of Alberta, Mr. Justice Julien Chouinard of the Quebec Superior Court and Mr. Justice D.V. Heald of Federal Court.

The transport department tests are to be examined by the commission when it resumes hearings in Montreal next month.

The report has not yet been made public by the department and officials of the Canadian Air Controllers Association and the Canadian Air Line Pilots Association said Thursday they won't comment on it until this is done.

However, Ken Maley, former president of the pilots, wrote in a union magazine that the tests proved "absolutely nothing."

Both the pilots and the controllers took part in the tests and the controllers are to attach their own views on the tests to the published report.

When the controversy raged in 1976—

prompting Jean Marchand to leave the Trudeau cabinet—the government promised Parliament would have the last say in the matter.

Otto Lang said the commission's recommendations on bilingual air control services would be debated in the Commons and a free vote taken on whether it should be accepted.

The report says bilingual air control services for Mirabel and Dorval probably could be introduced about 11 weeks after they are approved.

However it would take seven to eight years to complete the bilingual services in all of Quebec because of a master plan within the transport department which includes expansion of airspace now controlled by Quebec units.

Says the report:

"The total cost of the expansion for bilingual aeronautical communications in the province of Quebec is estimated at approximately $12 million. The implementation of all these programs should be completed in the next seven to eight years."

OFFICIAL LANGUAGES ACT
The Toronto Star, *October 9, 1976*
Reprinted with permission –
The Toronto Star

**PRIME MINISTER PIERRE TRUDEAU IS THE TARGET OF
ENGLISH-CANADIAN WRATH AT FEDERAL LANGUAGE POLICIES**

Questions
1. Examine the English- and French-Canadian reactions to the air traffic control dispute. To what extent do you feel each of the two groups' reactions was based on
    (a) a factual understanding of the issue?
    (b) emotion?
    (c) lack of sufficient information?

2. Compare the English- and French-Canadian reactions to the dispute. What evidence is there to suggest that there was a "dialogue of the deaf"?

4
Canada's Official Languages Act and Quebec's Bill 101

This chapter examines two approaches to the language question: the Official Languages Act of 1969, passed by the Canadian federal Parliament, and the Charter of the French Language, Bill 101, passed by the Quebec National Assembly in 1977.

THE OFFICIAL LANGUAGES ACT, 1969

The Official Languages Act was passed almost unanimously by Parliament in 1969. The only opposition to this legislation came from a group of some eighteen Conservative Members of Parliament led by John Diefenbaker, former prime minister. It made English and French the two official languages in Canada and established the right for both French- and English-speaking Canadians to be served by the *federal* government in their own language. Where the number of French-speaking people in a district surpassed a designated minimum, the government would establish bilingual services for Canadians in federal areas such as income tax, customs, baby bonuses, and the post office. The federal civil service began language programs for its employees. The use of French was expanded in most areas of public communications (for example, the CBC), and translation services with the federal government were greatly expanded.

The debate in the federal Parliament preceding the passage of the Official Languages Act had shown remarkable consensus in favor of the new policy among the three major national parties represented in Ottawa and of Social Credit with its MPs from Quebec. In spite of the initial opposition of John Diefenbaker and a group of Conservative MPs, which was recorded on second reading of the Bill, this group did not vote on final reading against the recognition of French as an official language. The final Bill had the support of the Liberals, Conservatives, New Democratic Party (NDP), and the Créditistes from Quebec. This is clearly reflected in the statements of the leaders of the three major parties: Pierre Trudeau for the Liberals, Robert Stanfield for the Conservatives, and David Lewis for the NDP. The following extracts from the House of Commons Debates indicate this official support of the policy of bilingualism.

Whatever happened later in rejection of this policy in English Canada in particular, including the policy of multiculturalism adopted in 1971, should be seen in the light of this original unanimity among the political parties.

EXTRACTS FROM HOUSE OF COMMONS DEBATES

October 17, 1968:

Pierre Trudeau: . . . We believe in two official languages and in a pluralist society, not merely as a political necessity but as an enrichment. We want to live in a country in which French Canadians can choose to live among English Canadians and English Canadians can choose to live among French Canadians without abandoning their cultural heritage.

Those of use who have some experience of the difficulties and opportunities of this course are conscious of the risk. But we are convinced that, as a country and as individuals, we must take it. French Canada can survive not by turning in on itself but by reaching out to claim its full share of every aspect of Canadian life. English Canada ought to attempt to understand this, and I believe it is doing so to an increasing degree. English Canada should not, of course, attempt to absorb French Canada. All Canadians should capitalize on the advantages of living in a country which has learned to speak in two great world languages. (p. 1481)

Robert Stanfield: Mr. Chairman, as leader of Her Majesty's Loyal Opposition I wish to say that I and my colleagues will vote in favour of this resolution which asks the house to agree, and we do agree, to the presentation of a bill which would officially designate English and French as the official languages of this parliament and of the government . . . (p. 1484)

David Lewis: . . . I look upon the measure which the resolution forecasts in the light both of our country's history and of its future. I regard this measure as redressing a profound oversight which has haunted Canadians for the first century of our existence as a country, an oversight which has harmed harmonious development among the citizens of this nation. I consider it as a step long overdue . . .

I say to my fellow Canadians whose mother tongue, like mine, was neither English nor French that this country is a bilingual country, that Canada is a country of mosaic design and is not a melting pot. I say to my fellow Canadians with origins other than English or French that it is precisely because Canada is a bilingual country, and has always been, that communities in Canada with languages and cultures other than English and French have been able to develop within economic, intellectual and moral concepts much higher than such communities have achieved in any other country in the world . . . (pp. 1486–1487)

– Canada, Parliament, *Debates* (House of Commons), Volume II, 1968 (Ottawa: Queen's Printer, 1969)

May 16, 1969:

Robert Stanfield: Mr. Speaker . . . This bill is placed before the house to strengthen rather than weaken Canadian unity. It is put forward for the purpose of making Canadians, whether they speak English or French, feel at home in this country to the extent that this is practical, and making federal government services available in the two languages. This is the principle which was discussed at the resolution stage. It was warmly accepted by all parties, including the New Democrats and Creditistes. Our task now is to judge the bill in the terms of these general purposes.

The purpose of this bill is not to compel English-speaking Canadians to learn French, and vice versa. This bill is aimed at providing French-speaking or English-speaking minorities with all federal government services in the language of their choice, as far as it is practical. If the purpose of this bill were to impose bilingualism, I would oppose it, as I believe virtually every member of this house would. (p. 8790)

– Canada, Parliament, *Debates* (House of Commons), Volume VIII, 1969 (Ottawa: Queen's Printer, 1969)

Keith Spicer, who was Commissioner of Official Languages for six years, described the Official Languages Act as follows:

It's a federal law supported by all parties and passed by Canada's Parliament in 1969 to establish the equality of the English and French languages in all federal institutions: that means government departments, Crown corporations and agencies – everything that's federal. With flexibility broadly geared to need, the Act sets out general principles and specific ways for achieving this equality. In simple terms it seeks to realize equality of status, rights and privileges for the two languages as languages of service by federal institutions to their "publics" and as languages of work within those institutions. In this light, English and French are the "official" languages of Canada.

– *Twenty Questions . . . And a Few More on Canada's Official Languages* (Ottawa: Office of the Commissioner of Official Languages, October 1973), p. 1

With the adoption of bilingualism, a new and equal policy seemed to be forming; while no anglophone would be forced to learn French, the bilingual policy meant that the use of French would be available to francophones in all major federal institutions.

Many hoped that the passing of the Act would solve one of Canada's age-old problems – tension between the French and the English in Canada. Many English-speaking Canadians were eager to learn French and language programs mushroomed across the country. This glowing vision of harmony between Canada's two founding peoples proved, however, to be illusory.

The disadvantages facing French Canadians did not disappear. Many Quebeckers came to view the official bilingual policy as "too little – too late" in the light of the major problems revealed by the report of the Commission on Bilingualism and Biculturalism.

The publications of the Royal Commission on Bilingualism and Biculturalism between 1965 and 1970 made many people aware of the disadvantages French Canadians, as "equal partners" of Confederation, had experienced for years. The Commission's reports demonstrate that, as a group, they were among the lowest paid in Canada. One finding showed that in Quebec, a unilingual, English-speaking Canadian of British origin was likely to earn about 20 to 25 percent more than a bilingual French Canadian.

Thus, for many reasons, the hope of bilingualism did not last long. Almost immediately complaints began to be heard that the program was too expensive. Many government employees resented being told they had to learn French if they wanted to advance to higher paying jobs designated bilingual. Although eager to receive language training, some found it difficult while others complained it was of little use in their work once they had become bilingual.

People in many parts of Canada opposed the Act on the erroneous basis that it would force French on the English-speaking populace at large. What they had not considered is the fact that, except for the civil service, the Act encourages unilingualism in that either English or French minorities may converse with the government in the language of their choice. Further, the Act was to have limited impact on the public insofar as it affected neither the provincial governments, nor municipal governments, nor private industry.

"A STEP FORWARD"
By Prime Minister Pierre Elliott Trudeau

"Why are they forcing French down our throats?"

That question has been asked by English-speaking Canadians who are concerned about the government's bilingualism policy and about the Official Languages Act which was recently enacted by Parliament.

The question is based on a widely shared misunderstanding of what our policy on bilingualism means. In fact, everyone in Canada will not be required to speak French, any more than everyone will be required to speak English.

You can grow up in parts of Quebec and never use English a day in your life. You can live in many parts of the country and never hear a single word of French. Most of the people who deal with the government of Canada speak only one language. It is because everyone in the country is not expected to speak both languages, and never will be, that the federal government must be able to speak to Canadians in either French or English wherever there are enough French speakers or English speakers to justify it.

Nothing is more important to a person than to understand and to be understood. The most common and the most effective tool we can use for this purpose is our language. Any policy which affects such an important aspect of our lives is bound to stir up some controversy.

But we should not mislead ourselves into magnifying the problem.

One of our country's great strengths is the spirit of mutual understanding and tolerance that motivates Canadians. I feel certain that the great majority of our people accept and respect the differences that exist among Canadians – differences not only of language but of religion, color and origin.

Nevertheless, some misconceptions have certainly arisen, and I am grateful for this opportunity to deal with a few of them.

For example, some people claim that the Official Languages Act will result in discrimination against those whose mother tongue is neither English nor French.

This is one of the most widespread and the most unjustified misconceptions. The Act itself states categorically that the rights and privileges of any language other than English or French, whether acquired by law or by custom, will in no way be diminished as a result of the Act. For instance, the right of people who do not understand English or French to be heard in court through an official interpreter will be maintained throughout this country.

The recognition of two official languages in no way alters the position of people whose ethnic origin is neither British nor French. Indeed, the Act has nothing to do with ethnic origins or cultural origins. As Canadians we believe that the diversity of our cultural backgrounds is a great national asset.

It is an enrichment for all of us that many of our citizens and their ancestors have come from Germany and Italy, Poland and the Ukraine, China and Japan, the Philippines and the West Indies, and so many other corners of the globe. We encourage Canadians of every background to preserve the values and traditions of the homelands in many ways, including grants for cultural events and organizations.

It would obviously be impractical for the government itself to operate in every language spoken by a group of Canadians. For practical purposes, the government's working languages must be those spoken by Canada's two major language groups, which between them make up the majority of our population . . .

– quoted in Alexander Hewlitt, *Separatism*, Canadian Issues Series (Toronto: Maclean-Hunter, 1971), pp. 48–52

Some westerners objected to such things as bilingual signs in national parks and bilingual labelling regulations.

Look at this bag of chips. French words all over it. Look at this word "croustilles"; what in hell does that mean? I had to taste them to find out that they were plain and not B-B-Q chips.

– *The Toronto Star*, October 9, 1976

Most people in the western provinces had lost patience with the federal bilingual program.

. . . French classes at St. Boniface College outside Winnipeg operated with a marginal enrolment of about 300 students prior to publication of the Bilingualism and Biculturalism Report in 1968.

After the B and B Report came out there was a sudden interest among English-speaking Canadians to learn French. Enrolment jumped to 3,000 and then doubled to 6,000. Now, enrolment is back at 300.

– *The Toronto Star*, October 9, 1976

Media reports showed that westerners were sick of having French "rammed down their throats." Disillusionment with the official bilingual policy often seemed more of an emotional response than a reaction based on actual inconveniences or infringements.

Some supporters of the federal government's bilingualism policy maintained that the program had been misunderstood by many Canadians. For example, one man in St. Pierre, Manitoba, mistakenly described bilingualism as follows:

My understanding of it is that a French guy can come into my general store and demand to be served in French. If I can't do it, I'm breaking the law.

– *The Toronto Star*, October 9, 1976

Or another person from British Columbia who said:

I don't mind federal offices using English and French in Quebec . . . but I get mad thinking of money spent so that someone on holiday out West can buy stamps from a French-speaking clerk for postcards to send back to Quebec.

– *The Globe and Mail*, Toronto, July 5, 1976

Another misconception some English Canadians had is that nearly all francophone Quebeckers are strong supporters of bilingualism. Actually, many Quebeckers feel that it is a scheme that does not overcome the problems of increasing cultural and linguistic assimilation that they are facing. Until the PQ took over the government of Quebec most new immigrants to the province had chosen to learn English as the main means of career advancement. For many French-speaking people, the official bilingualism policy seemed to avoid the major issues and concentrate on such minor reforms as bilingual stamps and cheques. As time went on, incident after incident indicated that Canada, rather than becoming bilingual, appeared to be developing into two unilingual nations within the same state.

Although the Canadian federal state had defined itself as bilingual, this policy had not prevented all of the provinces, except New Brunswick, from remaining essentially unilingual. Although the provinces granted their French minorities some bilingual education, they did not adopt provincial legislation similar to the federal government's Official Languages Act. They did not become bilingual, as Quebec had always been, nor did francophones achieve country-wide rights to French education (apart from New Brunswick) equal to the English education rights enjoyed by Quebec's anglophones.

The program of bilingualism had not met its original expectations. As we look at the disillusionment over bilingualism, as in the air traffic control dispute of 1976, it is important to be conscious of the *reactions* to the bilingual policy.

The air traffic control dispute of 1976 occurred after a debate about bilingualism in the federal civil service had been under way for over five years. The air traffic control dispute becomes clearer in the context of the more general debate over bilingualism, and the reactions to the federal bilingual policy, in turn, are easier to understand in the context of a history of numerous unresolved problems between English and French Canadians.

Was the air controllers' dispute to be the last straw on the back of the bilingual camel? Pierre Trudeau, who entered federal politics in 1965 claiming he would help save Confederation by gaining acceptance for official bilingualism from coast to coast, was saying in 1976 and 1977 almost exactly the same things he had said eleven years earlier. Without bilingualism Canada, as a country which included Quebec, could not exist, and Quebec should set an example to the rest of the country. English-speaking Canadians should be open-minded and consider the future of Canada; Quebec would surely separate if bilingualism was defeated. After a decade the push for bilingualism seemed to be where it was at the beginning.

> If the Government chose to force French-speaking pilots to learn English, "then I don't think Quebec would want to stay in the country." ... they will say "Well this is basically the separatist issue. If we can't operate even within our own province in our own language, then what the hell are we doing in this country?"
>
> – Pierre Trudeau, quoted in Richard Cleroux, "Quebec Outrage Builds Against Air Agreement," *The Globe and Mail*, Toronto, July 3, 1976

In this never-ending clash over federal bilingualism, Quebec's unilingual Bill 101, and the unilingual policies (in practice) of other provincial governments, we see a continuation of the dispute over the language of air traffic control. This debate on bilingualism versus unilingualism is still with us as part of the debate over whether Quebec will or will not remain in Canada. Like so many issues that have arisen between French- and English-speaking people in Canada, it is still unresolved.

— The Globe and Mail, Toronto, July 23, 1976

Questions
1. In your reading of the excerpts from the House of Commons Debates regarding the Official Languages Act, do you find any major differences in the views of the leaders of the three main political parties?

2. Keith Spicer, the former Commissioner of Official Languages, remarked that the Official Languages Act ought not to be criticized for taking anything away from anyone — that in fact it added rights. Assess this interpretation.

3. Write to the Commissioner of Official Languages regarding current policies and programs for which he is responsible.

BACKGROUND TO QUEBEC'S BILL 101

Disputes over the language of air traffic control and over the Official Languages Act of 1969 are, as we have seen, only the latest incidents in a long series of differences between the two founding national-cultural communities of Canada. Both these issues have been characterized by a virtual lack of communication between the two sides. We have viewed both sides of the air controllers' dispute and some of the debate in English Canada surrounding the federal official languages policy; now let us turn to Quebec's response to federal bilingualism.

LUNDI 8 SEPTEMBRE 1975 / JOURNAL DE MONTRÉAL

– Reprinted with permission of the artist, Rolland Pier

As mentioned earlier, the 1950s and 1960s in Quebec were a time of rapid changes in Quebec's economy, politics, and public opinion. The French-speaking community went through a process of self-definition that is often referred to as the "Quiet Revolution." Quebeckers began to see themselves in the context of an ever-changing industrial society and wanted to know more about where they stood.

Three important studies of the last fifteen years have been instrumental in drawing attention in Canada to a need to "redress the balance" between the two founding peoples. These were the Laurendeau–Dunton Royal Commission on Bilingualism and Biculturalism, the Parent Royal Commission of Inquiry on Education in the Province of Quebec, and the Gendron Commission of Inquiry on the Position of the French Language and Language Rights in Quebec.

The findings of these studies demonstrated that, as a group, people whose mother tongue was French: (1) were under-represented at all levels in the government of Canada; (2) received less education; (3) had higher infant mortality rates; (4) were lower in the salary scale (even in predominantly French-speaking Quebec); (5) entered professional careers less frequently; (6) had fewer health and social services available to them; and (7) had higher unemployment rates. The list seemed endless. Francophone Quebeckers had their suspicions confirmed and they were shocked. Here was strong evidence that they were a disadvantaged people whose very existence seemed threatened.

Over 75 percent of the five million francophones in the province of Quebec speak or understand no language other than French. Thus, the existence of a healthy and viable French language is extremely important to them. French is the language they use to express themselves, to communicate, and to make their living.

Lac Marois, May 20, 1970, Midnight

I always wondered why English-speaking Canadians appeared so shocked when we told them that we were like strangers in our own land. Our language, one of the first ever spoken on this continent, was for years thought of as a foreign language in most high schools in Canada! I am told it is no longer so; bravo!

I understand why Maritimers and Westerners balk at being obliged to learn French; maybe they really don't need to master a second language in this country. Québécois are not offended if they prefer to remain unilingual. After all many French-speaking Canadian nationalists refuse to learn English. It is their loss as it is for any human being, no matter where he lives, to close his eyes and his ears to the wonders and the beauty of another culture. But I am still unable to forgive our English Quebeckers for having lived for more than a century among us while haughtily ignoring our way of life.

– Solange Chaput-Rolland, *The Second Conquest; Reflections Two* (Montreal: Chateau Books, 1970), pp. 145–46.

It is evident that to be deprived the opportunity of complete expression in one's natural language is to be denied realization of one's personal and collective identity. If the consequences of this process of identity erosion — alienation and frustration — appear in a federal system such as Canada, or in a multi-ethnic province such as Ontario, the likelihood of the development of a vigorous national or provincial consciousness is seriously jeopardized.

"If I am not allowed to speak my own language in my own country, what am I but an immigrant. Our traditions and history will slowly be forgotten, our language lost, sooner or later we will be sucked into the rest of North America."

– quoted in Bill McGraw, "The Struggle to Keep the Fleur-de-lis Blooming in the City of Roses," *Detroit Free Press,* weekend supplement, June 1, 1975, p.11

THE THREAT TO THE FRENCH MAJORITY IN QUEBEC

A study done by the Quebec government in 1973 found that if current trends continued not only would the number of French-speaking people outside the province decline, but the number of people speaking French *in* Quebec and in Greater Montreal (where about half of Quebec's population lives) would also decrease. New immigration into Quebec since 1945 has posed a long-term threat to French as the language of the majority.

Several major reasons explain the threat to the French language in this country. The historical connection with France was interrupted by the Conquest. The military defeat of the French by the British in 1759 made English the main language of business and government in Canada, and for the most part in Quebec, too. Although the Quebec Act of 1774 recognized that the territory of Quebec was French-speaking and had its own customs and laws, the rights this Act established in theory did not always manifest themselves in practice.

Bilingual Country, Unilingual Citizens.

As an indication of the extent to which French has only recently begun to acquire a certain status in Canada, it might be recalled that even the provincial civil service of Quebec used English as the language of work during the 19th Century. The public utilities of Quebec became bilingual only after a vigorous campaign by the young French-Canadian nationalists of the day, in 1910, and most private industry still uses English as the major (if not the sole) language of internal communication. Outside Quebec, of course, French would hardly ever be used in factories or offices . . .

> – Richard J. Joy, *Languages in Conflict: The Canadian Experience,* Carleton Library No. 61 (Toronto: McClelland and Stewart, 1972), p.51

For two hundred years Quebec has been dominated by English-Canadian business interests. During the nineteenth century English was the working language of the civil service in Quebec. In business, French has tended to be the language of inferior jobs and low incomes while English has been the language of those with the higher executive positions.

English has been required for communication and promotion. As a special inquiry of the Gendron Commission noted in 1972:

> Both language groups (French and English) agree that at the upper management level, there is little room for French, . . . the common underlying opinion detected is that while there is a place for French at the bottom of the hierarchical ladder . . . there is much less at the intermediate levels and just about none at all at the top.
>
> – *Report of the Commission of Inquiry on the Position of the French Language and on Language Rights in Quebec,* Book I: The Language of Work (Quebec: Government of Quebec, 1972), p.132

The Preliminary Report of the Royal Commission on Bilingualism and Biculturalism, sometimes referred to as the Laurendeau–Dunton Commission, related similar findings:

> Everyone knows that here (Chicoutimi), where the population is 98% French Canadian, big business has made English the working language; anyone who wants to work his way up at the plant has to use English.
>
> – (Ottawa: Queen's Printer, 1965), p.77

Thus, in Quebec, where the language of the majority is French, many people "hang their language up with their coats" when they get to work. To achieve promotion or to get certain types of jobs they have to learn English.

In the early 1970s another Gendron committee studied the use of French in the work world. French-speaking employees who work almost exclusively in English felt that there were numerous obstacles to an increased use of French, even where the majority of fellow-workers were francophone. Some of these problems were fear of blocked promotion, fear of losing one's job, and fear of being isolated at work.

In 1969, for the first time, the Quebec government responded to the forces which threatened the position of the French language in Quebec. Bill 63 focussed on language rights in the school system and was the object of widespread controversy. Thousands of French Canadians took to the streets to protest what they saw as essentially a policy that aided the assimilation process that was threatening the French language.

As a result of the growing nationalism in Quebec the Liberal government of Robert Bourassa proposed new language legislation for Quebec. In 1974 the Quebec National Assembly passed Bill 22 — the Official Languages Act of Quebec. It was hoped this Bill would solve many of the problems that concerned Quebeckers about increasing assimilation.

Bill 22 made French the obligatory language of education unless children were already proficient in English. Only then would they be allowed to attend English schools. Besides making French the primary language of education, Bill 22 also proclaimed French the official language of the province of Quebec.

But, from the beginning, the Bill was surrounded by controversy. The strongest reaction again came in the area of language of education rights.

Some Quebeckers, particularly members of the PQ, did not support Bill 22 because they said it did not do enough to halt the decreasing use of French in Quebec and was full of concessions to the English language.

On the other hand, the anglophone community in Quebec believed that Bill 22 had deprived them of long-established rights or privileges in Quebec, particularly in education. Strong objections from anglophone Quebeckers continued through 1974 and 1975. In 1976 English Quebeckers were still campaigning against the section of Bill 22 which required the "testing" of children of immigrants for fluency in English to determine their competence in the language.

BILL 101

Upon assuming office, the Parti Québécois, because of the importance of the language issue to francophone Quebeckers and in view of its own active role in movements to strengthen the status of French, introduced new language legislation. This was Bill 101 — the Charter of the French Language — which became law in September 1977.

The purpose of the Bill is to create a Quebec which is basically unilingual (French) just as eight other Canadian provinces are essentially unilingual (English).

In Bill 101 (later Bill 1), "official language" refers to the ability and right of a person living in Quebec to work and communicate publicly in French. The Bill requires that all businesses in Quebec eventually make French the language of work. All signs in public places for stores and restaurants must also be in French if another language is used. Because this legislation conflicts with the goals of the federal bilingual program, much controversy has resulted.

For the first time in Quebec there was now a law which proclaimed that every Quebecker has the right to work and to receive his education in French. Public administration, health and social services, professional corporations, and employees' associations were now obliged to inform and serve in the French language.

Bill 101
Charter of the French language
Preamble

WHEREAS the French language, the distinctive language of a people that is in the majority French-speaking, is the instrument by which that people has articulated its identity;

Whereas the National Assembly recognizes that Québecers wish to see the quality and influence of the French language assured, and is resolved therefore to make of French the language of Government and the Law, as well as the normal and everyday language of work, instruction and communication;

Whereas the National Assembly intends in this pursuit to deal fairly and openly with the ethnic minorities, whose valuable contribution to the development of Québec it readily acknowledges;

Whereas the National Assembly recognizes the right of the Amerinds and the Inuit of Québec, the first inhabitants of this land, to preserve and develop their original language and culture;

Whereas these observations and intentions are in keeping with a new perception of the worth of national cultures in all parts of the earth, and of the obligation of every people to contribute in its special way to the international community; . . .

– Quebec. National Assembly, *Bill 101: Charter of the French Language.* 31st Legislature, 2nd Session, 1977. (Preamble)

The considerable controversy that has arisen over Bill 101 has come mainly from anglophone Quebeckers. A majority of francophone Quebeckers support this Act, as evidenced by the almost unanimous support for the major features of the Bill received in the National Assembly. Even the Quebec Liberal party, in a convention held in November 1977, decided not to challenge Bill 101 in the next provincial election.

Bill 101 guaranteed an education in English to children whose father or mother had received his or her elementary education in English in Quebec, or whose father or mother, domiciled in Quebec on the date on which the Act came into force, had received his or her elementary education in English outside Quebec. However, most of the English-speaking population of Quebec objected to the principles outlined in the Bill. Specifically, they objected to how the Bill would affect them in their place of work, and to the enrolment in French schools of all children of immigrants to Quebec who were not already in English schools, and children of Canadian citizens who move to the province after the passing of the Act and who did not have a background of anglophone education in Quebec.

The predominant role of anglophones in business and the advantageous position long enjoyed by English-speaking employees were now challenged by Bill 101. Businesses in which English was the main language used were concerned about how they would implement the frenchification measures outlined in the new charter. Some head offices were threatening to move their operations out of Quebec primarily because of the passage of the Bill.

Immigrant groups were the most vocal in their opposition to the Bill, particularly with regard to the language of education. They were especially concerned about fellow members of their ethnic community who did not meet the requirements for English education outlined in the Bill.

Other immigrants in small businesses worried about their ability to serve the public in French. "I have come from Greece," one shopkeeper noted, "I can hardly speak English — I have no time to study French."

The heart of the debate around Bill 101 was a theme that has appeared repeatedly in all issues involving language rights in Canada — the theme of individual versus collective rights. The anglophone and ethnic groups in Quebec argued that as Canadian citizens they should have the freedom to choose between Canada's two official languages as established in the BNA Act of 1867 and in the federal Official Languages Act of 1969, while the francophone Quebecker majority held that the protection of French language and culture had priority over individual rights.

Questions

1. Is Solange Chaput-Rolland justified in saying, "... I am still unable to forgive our English Quebeckers for having lived for more than a century among use while haughtily ignoring our way of life."?

2. Is English the major language of business in Quebec? If foreign firms use German or French in Germany or France, is there any reason why English-speaking firms should not use the language of the majority in Quebec?

3. Bill 22, adopted by a pro-federal Quebec Liberal government, and Bill 101, adopted by a separatist PQ government, both proclaimed French as the official language of Quebec. What is the significance of this fact?

4. Does Bill 101 grant anglophone Quebeckers as much rights in education as Ontario grants to its francophones? What, if any, is the difference between the two situations?

5
Language of Education

> In a country like Canada the school must sooner or later become . . . the principal stake to be struggled for by the opposing forces, national and religious. . . . What is at issue is not merely the lot of a ministry, a party, a method of government, but the very destiny of two peoples and two civilizations.
>
> The problem of Canadian education is one of infinite complexity. . . . We have two separate races, living together under the same laws but not speaking the same language or practising the same religion. Each of these two races is so strongly attached to that which constitutes its individuality that it would not sacrifice the smallest particle of it to the cause of the unity of the nation.
>
> – André Siegfried, The Race Question in Canada (1906; reprinted ed., Toronto: McClelland and Stewart, 1966), p. 185

While conflicts between French and English Canadians have had many dimensions, the right to have one's children educated in either the English or the French language has been the issue in many disputes. Throughout Canadian history, the opposing themes of individual versus collective rights, discussed earlier, have converged on the educational systems of the provinces.

The agreement of 1867, which effected the federation of four separate colonies in British North America into one state, was possible only to the extent that it guaranteed the jurisdiction of provincial governments over education. One of the architects of Confederation, John A. Macdonald, summarized the situation which existed prior to the agreement to establish the new country:

> The . . . Lower Canadians [Quebec] drew themselves up and said, if the constitution were not drawn up so as to give them power to protect beyond a doubt, their institutions, their religion, their language, and their laws in which they had so great pride, they would never consent to a union, and if we had not agreed to that, we should not have had the Dominion of Canada.
>
> – J. A. Macdonald to Costigan, 1872, in Robert Sellar, The Tragedy of Quebec: The Expulsion of Its Protestant Farmers (1907; reprinted ed., Toronto: University of Toronto Press, 1974), p.184

In the fight for survival as a national-cultural community, French Canadians have fought hardest over the right to have their children — the inheritors of their language and culture — educated in their own schools in the French language. As implied in the quotation by André Siegfried, education is the arena in which reconciliation of individual–collective rights and minority–majority rights is most difficult. It is in the field of education, too, that the fragile nature of Canadian unity and federalism is tested.

A LONG HISTORY

After Confederation, most disputes concerned the extent to which the French-Canadian minorities outside Quebec were to enjoy rights similar to those afforded the English minority in Quebec. Central to these clashes was the main institution of cultural preservation — the school. The BNA Act supported the principle of denominational schools, but, on the whole, left educational legislation to the provinces. Section 93 of the Act, in reference to the educational rights and privileges enjoyed by the minority groups in both Canadas (that is, Ontario and Quebec) prior to 1867, deals with education solely in terms of religious denominations and not in terms of linguistic groups. Although the issue of Catholic schools was not specifically a bilingual issue, the right to denominational schools and the right to schools in which the language of instruction was to be French were linked. As one prominent Canadian historian has stated:

> While the constitution in some cases has protected religious separate schools in a limited way, it gives no protection to French language rights ... so where French-language schools existed by custom they have been eliminated by measures that are, according to the courts, within the letter of the constitution. Whether these measures are within the spirit of the constitution is a matter that neither the courts nor historians can decide with certainty....
>
> — Ramsay Cook, *Canada and the French-Canadian Question* (Toronto: Macmillan of Canada, 1966), p.149

THE BRITISH NORTH AMERICA ACT 1867

93. In and for each Province the Legislature may exclusively make Laws in relation to Education, subject and according to the following Provisions:—

(1). Nothing in any such Law shall prejudicially affect any Right or Privilege with respect to Denominational Schools which any Class of Persons have by Law in the Province of the Union:

(2). All the Powers, Privileges and Duties at the Union by Law conferred and imposed in Upper Canada on the Separate Schools and School Trustees of the Queen's Roman Catholic Subjects shall be and the same are hereby extended to the Dissentient Schools of the Queen's Protestant and Roman Catholic Subjects in Quebec:

(3). Where in any Province a System of Separate or Dissentient Schools exists by Law at the Union or is thereafter established by the Legislature of the Province, an Appeal shall lie to the Governor General in Council from any Act or Decision of any Provincial Authority affecting any Right or Privilege of the Protestant or Roman

Catholic Minority of the Queen's Subjects in relation to Education:

(4). In case any such Provincial Law as from time to time seems to the Governor General in Council requisite for the due Execution of the Provisions of this Section is not made, or in case any Decision of the Governor General in Council on any Appeal under this Section is not duly executed by the proper Provincial Authority in that Behalf, then and in every such Case, and so far only as the Circumstances of each Case require, the Parliament of Canada may make remedial Laws for the due Execution of the Provisions of this Section and of any Decision of the Governor General in Council under this Section.

– Revised Statues of Canada, 1970, Appendices
(Ottawa: Queen's Printer, 1970), pp. 217–18

Against this background were waged at least two critical disputes in the late nineteenth and early part of the twentieth century. Although the spirit of Confederation was still young, provincial governments embarked on policies designed to restrict the rights of their French-Canadian citizens.

Questions

1. André Siegfried remarked in 1906 that "the two races [English and French] are not willing to sacrifice...." How appropriate do you feel this comment is today?

2. Re-read John A. Macdonald's letter to Costigan. How might John A. have reacted to Bills 63, 22, and 101?

SOURCES OF CONFLICT

The union of the colonies in British North America — Canada West, Canada East, Nova Scotia, and New Brunswick — had been declared by many, although disputed by others, to have established a framework within which the two "founding peoples" could work out a common destiny while at the same time maintaining their individual distinctiveness. Confederation, it was argued, had been made possible by the willingness of the colonies to subordinate their regional needs and autonomy to those policies and programs which would be of mutual benefit to the partners. The spirit of optimism, accord, and accommodation of the Confederation period was, however, to be short-lived.

The immediate task which confronted the new dominion involved territorial expansion — the construction of a transcontinental nation. The central government demonstrated concern over the future of the vast area to the west of Ontario. It was felt that Canada must expand its boundaries westward if the new country was to ensure its own destiny. By 1869 the government of Canada had successfully negotiated with the British government the transfer of the lands of the Northwest from the Hudson's Bay Company to its own administration. It was intended that Ottawa would provide the area with a temporary government to be replaced once the status of the lands within the federal union was decided.

The failure of the federal government to consult the settlers of the Northwest regarding their future status or to suggest the type of status likely to be granted generated a feeling of mistrust and frustration within the Red River area. Many of the ten thousand people feared that their right to occupy and use lands in the "unsettled areas" would be denied unless

Ottawa made provision for ownership by tradition as well as freehold tenure. Other issues included the degree to which the settlers would participate in local government and the guarantee of language rights for both the French-speaking and English-speaking populations.

Table 2/ Population Characteristics, 1870 (Rupert's Land)

White Settlers	1,565
French-speaking Métis	5,756
English-speaking Métis	4,083
Indians	558

Source: Peter Charlebois, *The Life of Louis Riel* (Toronto: NC Press, 1975), p.26

The transfer of the territory was to take effect on December 1, 1869, yet by September the federal government had still not made an effort to involve the residents of the area in the formulation of the conditions of the transfer. As a consequence, settlers, under the leadership of Louis Joseph Riel, established the National Committee of the Métis of Red River to make representations to the government. Among the committee's objectives was the recognition of the right of the Métis to participate in government and the continuation of language rights enjoyed by the settlers. The committee seized control of the administrative centre of the territory — the Hudson's Bay Company post at Fort Garry — and established a "provisional government" which would negotiate directly with the government in Ottawa.

The "provisional government," in an attempt to demonstrate its authority, refused admittance to the area to a group of surveyors under contract to the federal government. Among those arrested was Thomas Scott, a Protestant from Ontario. Scott escaped custody and unsuccessfully attempted to "take" Fort Garry. He was arrested once again in 1870 and imprisoned. While in jail Scott continued to resist the authority of the "provisional government" — he attacked the guards, insulted the Métis, and threatened to have Riel assassinated. As a result, Scott was charged with insubordination and taking up arms against the "government." Following a trial, Scott was executed.

The execution of Scott inflamed the animosity between English and French throughout the Dominion. In Ontario, the Orange Lodge, building on anti-French and anti-Catholic sentiment, pressured the government of Ontario into posting a reward of five thousand dollars for Louis Riel "dead or alive."

Developments within the Red River area impressed on Macdonald's government the need to finalize the "terms of the transfer." Within a short period of time it was agreed that the territory would be admitted as a province — the Province of Manitoba. The constitution issued to the province declared that both English and French would be "official languages" and, furthermore, that the provincial school system would be a dual system with both Protestant and Catholic schools provided by the Manitoba government.

SOMETHING'S GOT TO GO SOON!

PETITION OF THE NATIONAL COMMITTEE OF THE MÉTIS REGARDING TERMS OF THE AGREEMENT, DECEMBER 1, 1869

1. That the people have the right to elect their own Legislature...

10. That the English and French languages be common in the Legislature and Courts, and that all Public Documents and Acts of the Legislature be published in both languages...

13. That we have a fair and full representation in the Canadian Parliament.

– Peter Charlebois; *The Life of Louis Riel* (Toronto: NC Press, 1975), p.44

DISPUTE OVER LANGUAGE OF EDUCATION IN MANITOBA

EXCERPTS FROM THE MANITOBA ACT, 1870

22. In and for the Province, the said Legislature may exclusively make Laws in relation to Education, subject and according to the following provisions:—

(1). Nothing in any such Law shall prejudicially affect any right or privilege with respect to Denominational Schools which any class of persons have by Law or practice in the Province of the Union:

(2). An appeal shall lie to the Governor General in Council from any Act or decision of the Legislature of the Province, or of any Provincial Authority, affecting any right or privilege of the Protestant or Roman Catholic minority of the Queen's subjects in relation to Education:

(3). In case any such Provincial Law, as from time to time seems to the Governor General in Council requisite for the due execution of the provisions of this section, is not made, or in case any decision of the Governor General in Council on any appeal under this section is not duly executed by the proper Provincial Authority in that behalf, then, and in every such case, and as far only as the circumstances of each case require, the Parliament of Canada may make remedial Laws for the due execution of the provisions of this section . . .

– Lovell Clark, ed., *The Manitoba School Question: Majority Rule or Minority Rights?* (Toronto: Copp Clark, 1968), pp.102–103

Immediately after joining the Union, Manitoba experienced considerable immigration. As a result, the composition of Manitoba's population changed and the distribution of the population between English and French which had existed prior to 1870 was altered. The recently arrived immigrants were predominantly English-speaking. By 1890, the Protestant and English majority expressed resentment over the dual educational system and the continued use of the French language. The Manitoba Liberal government of Thomas Greenway, conscious of the population changes and responsive to pressure from the majority group, introduced in 1890 legislation which was to remove the guarantees provided by the Manitoba Act of 1870 to the French and Catholic minorities.

The government embarked on a legislative program which restructured the educational system of the province. The dual system was replaced by a nondenominational system in which English was to be the only language of communication and instruction. To effect the establishment of a unitary system of education the government withdrew financial support from Catholic schools. The Catholic French Manitoban was outraged — not only had he been denied official status for his language but too he had been denied the right of sending his children to a denominational school which had assured not only a Catholic education but a French Catholic one. It was obvious that developments in the province presented a challenge to the nature and intent of the Manitoba Act. Increasingly it was realized that the challenge would call into question the very principles on which the federal union was established. Was the union of 1867 a partnership within which the two societies — English and French — were to enjoy equality? Was it the intention of those who drafted the British North America Act that the French should enjoy rights outside Quebec similar to those enjoyed by the English inside Quebec?

French Canadians across Canada watched the Manitoba question with deep concern. Quebec newspapers especially focussed on events in the West. For the French a fundamental assumption about the nature of their country had been attacked.

Developments in Manitoba also attracted the interest of many English-speaking Protestants in Ontario. To the Orange Lodges of Ontario the situation in the West provided evidence to support their widely publicized beliefs.

The minority in Manitoba appealed to the federal government to disallow the offensive legislation. It was argued that the legislation was contrary to the constitutional guarantees and warranted the intervention of the federal government which, in such cases, was empowered to disallow provincial legislation or to pass remedial legislation which would return constitutional provisions.

The governments of both Bowell (Conservative) and later Laurier (Liberal) were reluctant to be drawn into a conflict which pitted Catholic against Protestant, French against English. Thomas Greenway, premier of Manitoba, warned the federal government to remain outside the issue. Greenway argued that it was clearly within the province's authority, specified in the BNA Act, to make laws regarding education. In 1896 Laurier's Liberals won the general election and set about the conduct of government business. No longer could the fine legal points regarding the Manitoba Act be debated. Laurier attempted to reach a settlement which would not increase the animosity. Although Prime Minister Laurier persuaded the Manitoba government to provide limited educational and religious instruction in French where there were ten or more French-speaking students, the event was one of the most bitterly fought debates in the history of French–English relations. (In this connection it is interesting to note that on April 25, 1979, the Manitoba Court of Appeal handed down a unanimous judgment finding "inoperative" the 1890 Act. In its judgment, the Court found that the Manitoba Act of 1870 intended, in section 23, to give the French language in Manitoba the same protection that section 133 of the BNA Act gives to English in the courts and legislature of Quebec and to French in the federal courts and Parliament.)

In 1970, the Manitoba government passed Bill 113, giving back to French-speaking residents of that province the right to have their children educated in French, a right which they had enjoyed in 1870. After Bill 113 was enacted, only two major high schools in St. Boniface adopted the all-French curriculum. Most of the others opted for either half French and half English, or a single hour of instruction daily.

Just as the Manitoba Schools Question was being settled, Ontario moved toward the establishment of a unilingual system of education. Once again the two linguistic groups were pitted against each other. Once again reference was made to the historical evolution of the provincial school system and the intention or spirit of the provisions contained in the federal constitution.

In 1886 the *Toronto Mail*, in an article on Franco-Ontarians, characterized schools in which French was the language of communication as

> ... nurseries not merely of an alien tongue, but of alien customs, of alien sentiments and ... of a wholly alien people.

THE FRENCH LANGUAGE IN ONTARIO SCHOOLS

Ontario's educational system was rooted in educational policies established in the pre-Confederation period, especially during the years following the Act of Union in 1840. In Upper Canada (renamed Ontario in 1867) the system was to be basically nondenominational although provision was made for separate schools for the religious minority (primarily Roman Catholics). The distinction was perceived to be on the basis of creed, that is, religious beliefs, not tongue or language spoken. While it was assumed that the language of instruction and communication would most frequently be English, there had not been established any absolute policy. In fact a letter regarding this very issue sent by Egerton Ryerson, the province's Chief Superintendent of Education, to the Trustees of Charlottenburg on April 24, 1857, clearly recognized the linguistic rights of the French Canadians in Canada West (Ontario).

> ... as the French is the recognized language of the country as well as the English, it is quite proper and lawful for the trustees to allow both languages to be taught in their schools to children whose parents may desire them to learn both.
>
> – quoted in C. B. Sissons, *Bilingual Schools in Canada* (Toronto: Dent and Sons, 1917), p.27

By the time of Confederation there had developed three kinds of "separate schools" which received legislative grant money: those established for special linguistic groups (French, German, Gaelic, Algonkian); those established for special racial groups (Blacks, Indians); and those established for special denominational groups (Roman Catholic and Protestant). The growth of these special interest schools, while not guaranteed by statute, was not denied by law.

It was in the post-Confederation period that the linguistic rights of Franco-Ontarians became a hotly debated issue. During the first two decades of the twentieth century spokesmen for both communities assaulted one another with impassioned arguments oftentimes comprised of invective, recrimination, and racism.

Once again there was disagreement over the nature of Canadian society and the role to be assumed by the two ethnic groups. The BNA Act itself was invoked to defend opposing interpretations. Section 93 of the Act, in reference to the educational rights and privileges enjoyed by the minority groups in both Canadas prior to 1867, deals with education solely in terms of religious denominations and not in terms of linguistic groups. Writing in 1966, Ramsay Cook reflected on the nature of the federal constitution:

> ... one part of the French-Canadian community is left unprotected in practice if not in theory. These are the French-Canadians living beyond the frontiers of the mother province. While Quebec is a constitutionally bilingual province, the other provinces, except for a brief two decades in Manitoba, have been unilingual.... While the constitution in some cases (Ontario for example) has protected religious separate schools in a limited way, it gives no protection to French language rights...
>
> ... so where French-language schools existed by custom they have been eliminated by measures that are, according to the courts, within the letter of the constitution. Whether these measures are within the spirit of the constitution is a matter that neither the courts nor historians can decide with certainty.
>
> – Ramsay Cook, *Canada and the French-Canadian Question* (Toronto: Macmillan of Canada, 1966), p.149

Insofar as no specific statutory provision had been made in Ontario for the use in schools of any language other than English, the Department of Education — established in 1876 — encountered increasing pressure to ban all teaching in French. Evidence that English was not being taught in twenty-seven out of one hundred and forty-five classrooms surveyed in 1885 led to the enactment of a department regulation requiring the use in every room of "authorized Readers" — available only in English.

By 1890 the French and German schools were allowed to teach French or German reading and grammar, and composition as extra subjects. The movement toward a unilingual educational system culminated in 1890 with a regulation of the Ontario government which stated officially that English is the language of instruction and communication "except where impracticable by reason of the pupil not understanding English" (quoted in *Report of the Royal Commission on Education in Ontario*, Toronto: Baptist Johnston, Printer to the King's Most Excellent Majesty, 1950, p.401). The policy satisfied the Anglo-Saxon community's demand that the government legislate the cultural basis of the province. As the next two decades were to demonstrate, however, policy enforcement was much more difficult than policy generation.

Embittered, disillusioned, and disenchanted, Franco-Ontarians recognized that collective action must be taken if their identity as a cultural group was to be preserved. Gathering in Ottawa in 1910, one thousand representatives of Franco-Ontarians established the Association canadienne-française de education de Ontario (ACFEO) with the purpose of obtaining equal rights for the French language in Ontario. The Whitney government was advised that Ontario, like Quebec, should be a bilingual province providing educational equality for both French and English.

The development of the ACFEO as a political force championing the Franco-Ontarian intensified the reaction of two opposing groups, the Orange Lodge and the Irish Catholics. Normally unsympathetic to each other, Anglo-Saxon Protestants and Irish Catholics found common ground in combatting the spread of French language and culture in Ontario. The Irish Catholics, ever suspicious of the militant Protestantism of the Orange Lodge, recognized that any modification in the government's language policy would result in French Catholic opposition to Irish Catholic control of parish and school. United together, both groups mounted a campaign intended to bring to the government's attention examples of blatant defiance of the department's language policy.

The following excerpts present examples of such an attitude:

1. The Grand Orange Lodge of Ontario West resolved that:

The use of the French language in the Public and Separate Schools of Ontario constitutes a grave menace to the integrity of the province as an English speaking community. (...) Therefore we protest in the most solemn and emphatic manner against the special privileges which the French are granted by the regulations of the Education Department (...) and we respectfully request the Government of (...) Ontario to enact such laws and make such amendments to the regulations (...) as will make it unlawful and impossible for the French language to be used in any of the Public or Separate schools of (...) Ontario.

> – Grand Orange Lodge of Ontario West, Resolution, special dispatch to the *Mail and Empire,* Toronto, 1912

2. Robert Sellar in the *The Tragedy of Quebec: The Expulsion of Its Protestant Farmers* (1907; reprinted ed., Toronto: University of Toronto Press, 1974), pp.327–28.
"The issue . . . is fundamental and admits of no compromise, it is one that is not local but affects the future of the entire Dominion. It is simply whether this Canada of ours is to be British, and nothing else than British, or whether it is to be a mongrel land, with two official languages and rules by a divided authority. Should Ontario buckle under to the demand now being made upon her, farewell to the hope of Canada being British."

3. H.B. Morphy, Conservative MP.
"Never shall we let the French Canadians implant in Ontario the disgusting speech that they use."

> – Mason Wade, *The French Canadians, 1760–1967* (Toronto: Macmillan, 1968), p.670

4. *The Globe*, Toronto, February 26, 1916.
No one denies the right of the French-Canadian people to use their own language in the Legislature, courts, and schools *of the Province of Quebec.* They are self-governing in the Provincial sphere, and doubtless have a very large power to restrict and hamper the use of the English language if they are so minded. The *people of Ontario* do *not* concede that in this Province any rights were conferred on the French-Canadian people which

entitle them to regard French as an official language to be spoken at will in the Legislature, the courts, and the schools on an equality with English.

Ontario is not bilingual. There is but one official language, and that is English.

5. *Orange Sentinel,* Toronto, February 3, 1910.

It is part of the great ambition of the French that French be equal with English, should that demand ever be conceded . . . the battle waged for a century will have been lost, and the barrier that Ontario has so long opposed to the oncoming tide of French settlement will have been swept away. All that would mean to the destiny of Canada cannot be readily imagined. It would almost inevitably mean French domination and Papal Supremacy.

Facing increased pressure, the Department of Education directed that F. W. Merchant, Director of Technical and Vocational Education, conduct an investigation into the extent to which English had become the language of instruction and communication in the province's schools. The Report submitted in 1912 contained evidence which indicated that the department's 1890 policy was indeed being ignored.

The department responded by enacting Instruction 17 ("Regulation 17") which stated that, starting in the academic year 1912–13,

> Clause 3. French may be used as the language of instruction and communication; but such use of French shall not be continued beyond Form I . . .
> Clause 4. . . . instruction in French shall not interfere with the adequacy of the instruction in English . . . and shall not in any day exceed one hour in each classroom. . . .
>
> – quoted in *Report of the Royal Commission on Education in Ontario* (Toronto: Baptist Johnston, Printer to the King's Most Excellent Majesty, 1950), pp.423–24

Premier Whitney justified Instruction 17 by claiming that such a policy was in the best interests of the Franco-Ontarians, who needed an adequate understanding of English in order to function in the province. It was, Whitney argued, not a new policy but merely a formalization of existing policy.

Opposition to Instruction 17 was immediate and impassioned. The debate was carried from the schoolyard to municipal councils to the courts and, ultimately, to the League of Nations.

The controversy became a national catastrophe. Henri Bourassa, spokesman for many French Canadians, argued that Instruction 17 must be resisted:

> . . . because in destroying our language it will annihilate our race . . .
>
> – Robert Sellar, *The Tragedy of Quebec: The Expulsion of Its Protestant Farmers* (1907; reprinted ed., Toronto: University of Toronto Press, 1974), p.303

Bourassa added in *Le Devoir* on April 20, 1915:

> Let no mistake be made: if we let the Ontario minority be crushed, it will soon be the turn of other French groups in Canada.

Le Droit in an open letter to French Canadians overseas wrote:

You will soon find your wives and children and sisters in the trenches in Canada for the defence of their language and schools against the might of a persecuting government. You can therefore say with reason: "Of what use is it for us to fight against Prussianism and barbarity here when the same conditions exist at home."

– quoted in Robert Brown and Ramsay Cook, Canada, 1896-1921: A Nation Transformed (Toronto: McClelland and Stewart, 1974), p.258

Relations between English and French were strained further by the federal government's announcement of the "national Service Programme" early in 1917. Conscription, combined with Instruction 17, challenged the very foundation of the country.

TOO LATE!

A Solid Quebec Will Vote to Rule All Canada Only a Solid Ontario Can Defeat Them

LOYAL ELECTORS! VOTE FOR NO MAN WHOSE MONARCH IS THE POPE OF ROME. DEFEAT EVERY PAPISH CANDIDATE, ONTARIO PROTESTANTISM IS ON TRIAL (...) TODAY, WHILE PROTESTANTISM IS ASLEEP ON DUTY, AND FEEDING ITS VANITY UPON THE DRY HUSKS OF PAST ACHIEVEMENTS, ROME IS WORKING NIGHT AND DAY, LAYING ITS LINES, DIGGING ITS TRENCHES, AND MARSHALING ITS FORCES TO CONTROL THE POLITICAL SITUATION IN CANADA.

-The Menace, Weekly, Aurora, Ontario, Saturday, June 27, 1914, Ferguson Papers, P.A.O.

Quebec Must Not Rule All Canada

In 1925 Dr. Merchant was again invited to examine the province's educational system. The committee made a number of recommendations for improving the quality of "English–French Schools" which, for the most part, were given in a conciliatory and moderate tone. The recommendations suggested more intensive supervision of the schools and recruitment of better-trained teachers. By 1927 some concessions were made to the French Canadians concerning Instruction 17, but it was to remain in force to 1944. Although the resolution did grant French Canadians additional rights in the schools of Ontario, many echoed the criticism published in *Le Devoir* (September 22, 1927): "... French rights in Ontario are still not equal to English rights in Quebec."

It was only in the mid-1960s, after a greater awareness of bilingualism was stimulated by the bilingualism and biculturalism report, that significant modification of Ontario's language and education policy was made.

In 1968 legislation was passed which granted the right to establish "French" schools if the parents of twenty-five elementary school students (twenty at the secondary level) sent a petition to their board of education.

In spite of the legislation passed in 1968 some difficulties arose in the succeeding years. In 1969, for example, the Board of Education in Sturgeon Falls in Northern Ontario refused to build a French-language high school, even though requested to do so by the French-speaking citizens, who were in a majority. The Board claimed it did not have the money to finance construction. In the southeastern portion of the province, in Cornwall, the French community asked for a government-funded French-language high school. Its request was refused.

In order to resolve some of the problems raised in these areas, the government of Ontario established a commission to study the problem. As a result of the findings of the commission, the Education Act was altered and the language rights of Franco-Ontarians strengthened.

Since 1974 some incidents have occurred in Ontario concerning the education of francophones. The Windsor area (Essex) was the scene of protests by francophones. In Ottawa similar problems arose at Champlain High School. The law covering establishment of francophone schools is still very new, and many people have not accustomed themselves to the rights now being offered to Franco-Ontarians.

As of 1978 the official stand of the Ontario government was that it would not declare French an official language of the province for fear of a backlash from anglophones. Instead, the government said that it would proceed quietly and cautiously to make French-language education available wherever numbers and requests make such education desirable and feasible.

Questions
1. In your opinion, does the decision of the Manitoba Court of Appeal of April 1979 declaring the Act of 1890, which had abrogated the right of francophone Manitobans to an education in French, "inoperative" signify a change in Canadian public opinion, or is the decision strictly the result of legal considerations?

2. Have the anti-French opinions expressed by members of the Orange Order in Ontario in the early twentieth century become a thing of the past, or are such attitudes still widespread in English Canada? Do any of your acquaintances hold such attitudes today?

3. How does the status of French in education in Ontario differ today from that of the period 1910 to 1940?

4. Compare Ontario's Instruction 17 to Quebec's Bill 101. In your opinion which piece of legislation was more restrictive of the rights of the minority linguistic group (English-speaking in Quebec; French-speaking in Ontario)?

UNILINGUALISM AS POLICY OUTSIDE QUEBEC

At the end of the 1970s it appeared that Canada outside of Quebec, with the possible exception of New Brunswick, was destined to be unilingual. If assimilating the French, the goal of the Durham Report, had been abandoned as an official policy for Canada, confining French to Quebec appeared to be the unspoken policy of provincial governments. British Columbia, Alberta, and Saskatchewan all adhered essentially to a one-language school system with minor concessions, such as French-language lessons.

The policy of unilingualism outside Quebec was clearly demonstrated when it came to developing a policy concerning recent immigrants from Europe. The availability of language choice was rarely proposed. The adoption of the English language in education was assumed to be the only means of impressing a Canadian identity onto these newcomers:

> ... The task before us is to take this mass of people and educate them properly, which can only be adequately done by bringing them under the same educational system.
>
> – Clifford Sifton, Attorney General of Manitoba, at Massey Hall, Toronto, April 24, 1895, in Lovell Clark, ed., *The Manitoba School Question: Majority Rule or Minority Rights?* (Toronto: Copp Clark, 1968), p.81

Yet it must be recalled that Confederation was accomplished by ensuring linguistic and cultural rights for the French-Canadian citizens of the country. Indeed, as we outlined earlier, the BNA Act did establish French and English as the two official languages of Canada. Thus we must not let our discussion about language rights for French-speaking Canadians be confused with what is termed a "multi-cultural" perspective. It is true that Canada is made up of many ethnic communities; however, the rights of French-speaking people are not the same as minority rights of ethnic groups who have, since Confederation, helped build Canada. To view the French-language rights of over six million French-speaking people as "minority rights" is to misread the past.

> To ignore French as a living Canadian language, and officially recognized at the time the country was formed, or to lump it with other minority languages just because the numbers game happens to come out on the side of English speakers, it seems to me amounts to a rather ungenerous ignoring of historical and present-day political reality. Justice is surely not only a matter of numbers. Democracy does not mean that the majority has a right to crush the minority — or administer it linguistically out of existence.
>
> – Keith Spicer, former Commissioner of Official Languages, in "The Official Languages," *The Civil Service Review*, Vol. XLVI, No. 3 (Ottawa: September, 1973), p.6

6
The Winds of Assimilation: Francophones Outside Quebec

THE PRESENT SITUATION

One and a half million Canadians of French ethnic origin live outside Quebec in communities scattered from St. John's, Newfoundland, to Victoria, B.C. Many of these people, since they are located in environments in which English is the language of business, education, and social communication, sense even more than Quebeckers a need to protect their francophone heritage from assimilation. Some French Canadians have concluded that they are fighting a losing battle.

St. Boniface in Manitoba at one time was the home of over twenty thousand French-speaking people who could work and live using only French. Today the signs of assimilation are everywhere.

In commenting on the growing tendency toward geographical concentration on the part of Canada's English- and French-speaking populations, the Task Force on Canadian Unity wrote:

> Canada's French-speaking population is increasingly to be found in Quebec — in 1951, 82 per cent of Canada's French mother tongue population lived in that province; by 1976, this proportion had risen to 85 per cent and demographers have estimated that by the census of 2001, approximately 95 per cent of Canada's francophones will be located in Quebec. Within the province itself, formerly English-speaking communities outside of the Montreal area are becoming French-speaking due to the migration or assimilation of anglophones. There is evidence that the use of English in Quebec as a whole may be declining: the proportion of adult males in the province who speak English only has declined from 16 per cent in 1931 to 9 per cent in 1971, whereas the proportion who speak French only has risen from 34 per cent in 1931 to 45 per cent in 1971.
>
> – The Task Force on Canadian Unity, *A Future Together: Observations and Recommendations* (Ottawa: January 1979), pp. 46–47

One method of determining the degree to which French Canadians have lost contact with their culture and have been drawn into the prevailing milieu is to assess the extent to which they are able to use the language of their ethnic origin. The table which follows provides two sets of statistics relevant to the issue of assimilation. It shows the proportion of each province's population which is of French ethnic or cultural origin and the proportion in each province which identified French as the language learned in childhood and still understood ("mother tongue"). A comparison of the two suggests that a considerable number of French Canadians have lost fluency in the French language and have been effectively assimilated into an English environment.

Table 3 / Percentage Distribution of French as Mother Tongue and by Ethnic Origin in Canada and the Provinces, 1971

	French as Mother Tongue	French by Ethnic Origin
Canada	26.9	28.7
Newfoundland	0.7	3.0
Prince Edward Island	6.6	13.8
Nova Scotia	5.0	10.1
New Brunswick	34.0	37.1
Quebec	80.7	79.1
Ontario	6.3	9.6
Manitoba	6.1	8.9
Saskatchewan	3.4	6.1
Alberta	2.9	5.8
British Columbia	1.7	4.4
Yukon	2.4	—
Northwest Territories	3.3	—

Source: *Canada Year Book, 1976-77, Special Edition* (Ottawa: Statistics Canada, 1977), pp. 191-92. "French by Ethnic Origin" percentages based on Canada Year Book figures for 1971 and 1972, calculated by Wayne Jackson

The table shows that the following percentage of Canadians of French ethnic origin have lost fluency in the language of their ancestors: British Columbia, 61 percent; Alberta, 52 percent; Saskatchewan, 44 percent; Manitoba, 31 percent; Ontario, 35 percent; Newfoundland, 77 percent; Prince Edward Island, 53 percent; and Nova Scotia, 51 percent. In New Brunswick only 9 percent of people of French ethnic origin have lost fluency in French, while in Quebec the figure drops to about zero. Generally, the rate of loss of French is related to the distance from Quebec, and to the existence in these communities of a significant francophone population.

Some of those who have been effectively assimilated into the prevailing English-speaking environment echo Lord Durham in claiming that in order to take full advantage of opportunities in North America they must place primary emphasis on developing fluency in English. Others argue that the trend toward assimilation deprives a substantial number of one of Canada's founding peoples of an historic and natural right. To these Canadians the treatment meted out to francophones outside Quebec will determine the response of French Canadians generally to the question of what is their true homeland — Canada or Quebec.

Questions
1. Identify the provinces in which assimilation appears to be greatest. What factors or circumstances can you suggest which would contribute to a high rate of assimilation? What measures could be taken to minimize the impact of these factors?

2. "Without the protective shell of the rural French parish, the city-dweller is constantly exposed to the English language. His children will, almost invariably, learn the language of their English-speaking playmates and a high proportion of the French-origin adolescents will find themselves marrying partners who are of the same majority group; children of such couples may be able to understand both parents but would seldom choose French as their major language."

– Richard J. Joy, *Languages in Conflict: The Canadian Experience*, Carleton Library, No. 61 (Toronto: McClelland and Stewart, 1972), p.34

Do you agree with Joy's assessment? Do you believe that the assimilation of French Canadians outside Quebec is inevitable?

SURVEYING THE SCENE

The material which follows presents a sampling of regional sentiment regarding the status of francophones outside Quebec. As you read these excerpts identify the condition or circumstances which have affected the assimilation of French Canadians into English-Canadian culture.

1. OVERVIEW: "CROSS-CANADA CAMPAIGN"

2. PROVINCIAL SURVEY
   I. The West
   (a) British Columbia
   (b) Alberta
   (c) Saskatchewan
   (d) Manitoba
   (e) "A Growing Acceptance..."
   (f) "An Enormous Myth..."

   II. Ontario
   (a) Francophones Find Few Ontario Services
   (b) Filion Affair...
   (c) Letter to the Editor
   (d) Davis Kills Language Bill Hopes

   III. Anglophone Quebec

IV. Eastern Canada
(a) New Brunswick
(b) Nova Scotia
(c) Newfoundland

V. Summary
(a) "Most Provinces want English as Main Language"

I. OVERVIEW: CROSS-CANADA CAMPAIGN

The Montreal Star, *April 30, 1977*
© *The Montreal Star*

French Seeking Status

In Brockville, Ont., a French mental patient struggled into the psychiatric hospital desperate to talk to a doctor. Knowing no English, he was neglected because there are no French psychiatrists on staff, although a third of the patients are French.

In Cape Breton, the local chamber of commerce in French-speaking Ile Madame asked Nova Scotia highway minister Fraser Mooney for bilingual signs. "Too dangerous," he replied, and the French-speaking motorists were left to cope with English.

In Winnipeg, a French mother cried at a public meeting when she learned that the majority English Norwood school board refused the area's sizeable French minority an all-French school. "We have no French school rights," she lamented.

These and other examples of the lack of rights of minority francophone communities across the country have surfaced recently as the Federation of Francophones Outside Quebec began its nation-wide campaign to insist on better treatment from provincial governments.

While Quebec English supported by Prime Minister Trudeau protest the sudden curtailment of rights here, the federation — also with Trudeau's backing — is fighting for French Canadians in other provinces who it believes are floundering in forgotten corners.

The Parti Quebecois' celebrated French language charter has made francophone minorities elsewhere more conscious of their inferior position and more determined to rectify it.

Through the wave of publicity centred on Quebec's English community, the Federation of Francophones Outside Quebec has discovered that the English minority here is leagues ahead of them and will remain so even under new language legislation.

As a result the militant new organization is raising its sights in search of more French rights and services as the debate on Canada's shaky future warms up.

"Anglophones in Quebec may feel their rights are being reduced under the language charter," comments Paul Comeau of the Federation of Nova Scotia Acadians.

"But if we could win from our provinces what the English will retain under the new Quebec legislation, we'd dance in the streets."

Whether it concerns medical services, schools, media, traffic signs, legislatures or courts, Canada's one million francophones outside Quebec are becoming more and more aware they get shabby treatment.

This message came through clearly at a recent national conference in Winnipeg on bilingualism and multi-culturalism sponsored by the Canadian Council of Christians and Jews.

"In some respects the provinces treat us no better than ethnic groups," says Paul Comeau who, like most francophones, is dead set against multi-culturalism policies.

At the Winnipeg conference, Mr. Comeau and other francophones were shocked to discover that Westerners throw French into the multicultural grab-bag along with the Ukrainians, Germans, Mennonites and other post-confederation immigrant groups.

The effects of this disregard for the status of the French as a "founding people" is reflected in details of a recent report prepared by the Federation of Francophones Outside Quebec.

Entitled The Heirs of Lord Durham, the report catalogues the "broken dreams" of French-Canadians and shows how French outside Quebec has been plagued by galloping assimilation.

In 1971, 1,500,000 people outside Quebec claimed French origin. Yet only a million have French mother tongue and only about 700,000 use French regularly.

The position of Quebec anglophones, by contrast, has improved. Figures show that although only 640,000 are of English origin, 800,000 have English as a mother tongue and an additional 200,000 use English regularly.

French has been crushed throughout the country partly because the language is recognized in the legislature and courts of only one province: New Brunswick and only there for the past ten years.

Ontario goes so far as to allow francophones to speak French in the legislature, but it provides no back-up translation services.

Other provinces, such as Manitoba, which has had a historically strong French population, haven't made even this token gesture.

Manitoba, of course has had a history of ripping away French rights.

When the province entered Confederation, French and English were official in the legislature, courts and schools. In 1890 French parliamentary rights were dropped and in 1916 French schools were banned.

In Quebec, English has by law always had equal status with French in the legislature and the courts.

This is now changing. Under new language legislation the only official language of the legislature and courts will be French, and English will have no official status.

However, English individuals will still be able to address the national assembly, obtain translations of statutes, receive government services and go to court in English.

With the exception of New Brunswick, francophones elsewhere cannot use French to this extent.

The lack of school rights across the country has perhaps caused the most anguish in French communities because schools pass on and solidify a culture.

Only New Brunswick, Ontario and Manitoba give French schooling any official status, but even there, French schools are contingent upon school board whims and bureaucratic regulations.

In Essex county near Windsor, for example, a local major school board recently said "no" to French parents' requests for a French school.

For political reasons, the decision was overturned in special legislation by Premier Davis, but the next group of French parents may not be so lucky.

As francophone Ontario cabinet minister Jean-Jacques Blais said recently: "We are here on suffrage. Whatever we have is what the province has chosen to provide. French secondary schools could be abolished tomorrow at the whim of the Ontario government."

Past wounds over French school rights across the country remain vivid for most French-Canadians.

There have been problems in Sturgeon Falls, Cornwall and Galt in Ontario; St. Norbert, Taché, and now Precious Blood in Manitoba; Gravelbourg and Prudhomme in Saskstachewan; Bathurst and St. Jean in New Brunswick.

Some of the fights have been over demands for all-French schools.

Advocates explain that French classes conducted within English schools are next to useless because the children never become immersed in French and emerge less than competent in both languages.

2. PROVINCIAL SURVEY

I. The West

(a) BRITISH COLUMBIA

The Toronto Star, *October 9, 1976*
© *Claude Arpin/The Montreal Star*

Bilingualism: A Dirty Word in the West

Claude Arpin

KAMLOOPS, B.C.

The hottest thing on western Canadian radio stations this past summer wasn't a Johnny Cash hit. It was a piece of vitriolic anti-Quebec writing that originated from Brampton, Ont.

Entitled "Hey Quebec, go suck a lemon," the Brampton Daily Times article was picked up avidly by radio stations and weekly newspapers all across western Canada.

"It seemed to strike a responsive chord in our listeners," chuckled editorialist Jim Harrison, who read it over the three radio stations owned by NL Broadcasting of Kamloops, B.C.

He said he couldn't recall receiving more written requests from listeners for their own personal photocopy of an editorial.

Ms Ford, a native of Red Deer, Alta., wrote in the article: "Hey Quebec, go suck a lemon. Or better still, give me a divorce. A no-fault, no-contest, you keep your property, I'll keep mine.

"I don't want to be married to you any more, but hope we can stay friends because it would be nice to visit now and then. But the marriage just isn't working...."

"Let's have a heart-to-heart talk. I would love to speak French, but I don't want it shoved down my throat. I resent having to pay double for every label and package, but that's not really what gripes me.

"You've been talking to the next door neighbors, washing dirty laundry in public. You've made a global jackass out of the rest of us, thanks to your friends in Ottawa with the airport language issue....

"Quebec, you're the embodiment of everything I hate about minority groups.

"The whining, the yelling, the screeching about your rights with little concern for the rights of others. I'll let you in on a secret. Your rights end where mine begin and when you spit in my face, expect a reaction.

Bonjour, ami

"I quite simply don't want you anymore. Bonjour mon ami, find yourself a lawyer."

University of British Columbia education professor Marvin Lazerson estimates that the level of hostility towards Quebec has reached "enormous proportions."

"The feeling out here is that under no conditions could Quebec leave Confederation but if a number of nuclear reactors accidentally exploded and the province slid into the Atlantic, there would be great cheering."

The Globe and Mail. *Toronto, July 5, 1976*

BRITISH COLUMBIA: One Language, One Country

Malcolm Gray

Jack Ballander, a retired farmer, used the most common phrase: "French is being rammed down our throats. Believe me, I speak for everyone in B.C. when I say this."

* * *

"I don't mind federal offices using English and French in Quebec," Sidney Miles, an electrician said, "but I get mad thinking of money spent so that someone on a holiday out West can buy stamps from a French-speaking clerk for postcards to send back to Quebec."

Jacob Derksen, an unemployed first-aid attendant, said English should be the only official language in Canada. "One country, one language," he said, "Let the majority rule."

(b) ALBERTA

The Toronto Star, *December 4, 1976*
Reprinted with permission -
The Toronto Star

French is Alive and Well in the Prairies

Nicolaas Van Rijn

French-Canadian settlers came to the Prairies in the 1890s and the early 1900s, along with Ukrainians, Germans, Czechoslovakians, Hungarians, Dutch and Anglo-Saxons. Their children grew up speaking little or no English until they were well along in school – and then they acquired a tortured, heavily accented English that would be with them for the rest of their lives.

That generation decided their own children wouldn't have that language difficulty. So they saw to it that their children spoke only English at home.

There were exceptions – parents who insisted that their children grow up speaking both languages and aware of their full heritage. But it wasn't until the largely unilingual generation started bringing up families in the 1950s and early 1960s that they realized they'd been "short-changed" culturally. Parents began insisting that their children do what they couldn't – grow up speaking two languages.

Where French wasn't taught in school, the children were sent to private classes to learn the language of their grandparents. Cultural organizations, by then the preserves of the old, were revived and invigorated by the injection of youth. New ones were founded.

But, unaccountably, bilingual labelling appears to be polarizing more resentment against Quebec than anything else. It's as though the mere presence of French words on labels is an offensive insult to the average westerner.

Many are miffed because their own mother tongue – whether it be German or Ukrainian, or some other language – does not appear along with the English and French.

"We're the founding race out here," barks German-born Henry Lippert of Warburg, Alta.

"We built this part of the country, working 16 hours a day, seven days a week. Not the French. So why couldn't Ottawa recognize us as much as it recognized the French Canadians?"

A usually mild-mannered Seventh Day Adventist who teaches clarinet and saxophone to local schoolchildren, Lippert is one of an alarmingly large number of western Canadians whose hostility towards Quebec has been whipped up to a stage where it borders on pathological hatred.

"I'm a religious man," the 57-year-old machinist blurts out, "but I'm at the point now where I say let's take our guns and have it out with Quebec. If you win, we'll go back to the countries our parents came from but if you lose, you go back to France and we'll start over building a country that speaks only English."

To avoid war, however, Lippert firmly believes that Ottawa must disperse French-Canadian Quebeckers across Canada in the way Acadians were expelled from Nova Scotia by the British in 1755.

"There are lots of opportunities up north out here; they could homestead in places where we don't want to go and the government could even give them interest-free loans.

Learn English

"It would be hard at first but they would learn

English and after two generations they wouldn't even miss the French."

About 100 miles south of Warburg, in a town of 2,000 called Didsbury, Gordon Collie is waving a 25-cent bag of chips over his head.

"You wanna know how Ottawa is shoving French down our throats? Look at this bag of chips. French words all over it. Look at this word here, 'croustilles'; what in hell does that mean? I had to taste them to find out that they were plain and not B-B-Q chips."

Collie, 45, is the owner of the Didsbury Inn and like most Alberta wheat farmers who patronize his establishment, he is fed up with bilingualism.

"How would I feel if Quebec separated? Well, I'd feel good about it. Under the circumstances, it's the best thing that could happen to the country.

"Out West we wanted to keep Quebec in Confederation but in the last few years Trudeau has just gone too far and now we can't wait for Quebec to get the hell out."

The ruddy-faced, short-haired innkeeper feels that Albertans shouldn't be subjected to problems caused by bilingualism and should devote themselves to "real issues" such as attracting skilled workers to the labor-starved province.

But when asked if he feels Canada should relax its immigration policies, he reacts with horror:

"No, I don't think that's the answer; we've got enough Pakistanis in the country and some of them are even moving out here to Didsbury."

* * *

(c) SASKATCHEWAN

The Toronto Star, *December 4, 1976*
Reprinted with permission – The Toronto Star

French is Alive and Well in the Prairies

Nicolaas Van Rijn

"The English won over the French at the Plains of Abraham," she says, "so I don't see why it shouldn't be English everywhere in Canada.

"I don't feel the French are inferior to us but they sure act superior by wanting to break away from Canada and by trying to make us speak French."

* * *

If a French-Canadian westerner entertains any nationalistic notions, he had better not be too vocal about it, says 24-year-old Richard Marcotte, of Regina.

A student at the University of Saskatchewan's bilingual centre, Marcotte says he often has been told to "speak white" by fellow construction workers on various summer jobs.

"The English backlash is pretty much tied in with the level of education of English-Canadians. Construction workers, blue-collar workers and even some so-called professionals are mostly anti-French.

"The backlash is understandable in a way because a lot of these people were immigrants here 30 years ago and they were told to speak English. Now, Trudeau comes along and says the country is bilingual French and English. And there's no mention of their own mother tongue."

"We're Canadians first, then French Canadians. And that's how they should feel over there, too... Quebec would certainly be the loser if it goes."

In St. Isidore de Bellevue, 70 miles northeast of Saskatoon, they talk of visitors who think they've taken a wrong turn at a country junction and have ended up deep in rural Quebec, instead of in "just another Saskatchewan town."

Bellevue is six miles from the battlegrounds of the Riel Rebellion, and some of its French-Canadian settlers were there before 1885 when federal troops placed Louis Riel in custody for the last time.

Mederic Gareau's ancestors were in Bellevue in 1884, and Gareau, now 60, remembers growing up in a totally French environment. "We spoke French at home. We didn't know any English. All our neighbors were French, and everything at school was French," he says. "Things didn't change much for a long time."

* * *

Unlike other French-Canadian areas in Saskatchewan, Bellevue has remained culturally unadulterated. It is the last holdout against the ethnic mix of newcomers that has reduced the French population of other towns in the area to a minority.

For many years, Gareau says, isolation was the only reason the French communities on the Prairies stayed French.

Things changed with the introduction of television and of regional schools, with children from different backgrounds being bused in from a wide surrounding area.

As the regional schools become established in the 1960s, provincial education departments started designating some of them as French. In non-designated schools, French is offered only as a language option and instruction is limited to 30 or 40 minutes a day.

In designated schools, up to 50 per cent of the curriculum may now be taught in French, and in a few special cases, all instruction is in French and it's English that's taken as a language course.

(d) MANITOBA

The Toronto Star, *December 4, 1976*
Reprinted with permission – The Toronto Star

French is Alive and Well in the Prairies

Nicolaas Van Rijn

Tom Oleson, an editorialist for the Winnipeg Free Press, feels that Quebec's Bill 22 is in fact "killing bilingualism out here. It's giving the rednecks the kind of fodder they need to get people worked up."

* * *

Manitoba, with a proportionately higher French-Canadian population than either Saskatchewan or Alberta, already has 28 designated French schools, 11 of them in Winnipeg.

"It wasn't so long ago," recalls Roger Boucette of Winnipeg, "that it was actually illegal to teach French in Manitoba schools.

"If we want our children to speak another language," Boucette says, "we've learned that we've got to do it ourselves. The government can't do it, the community can no longer do it, so it's up to the family. And, with a bit of help from the schools – which we're now getting – I'm optimistic that we will continue to be aware of our heritage.

"At least, out here, there's no discrimination against us because we want our kids to know French. The Germans want their children to speak German, the Ukrainians want their children to speak Ukrainian, and when we all get together we can speak English with each other.

"That's very Canadian, isn't it?"

(e)
"A Growing Acceptance..."

The Sault Star, *Sault Sainte Marie,
Ontario, November 13, 1976
Reprinted with permission of
The Edmonton Journal*

by Guy Demarino

In The Edmonton Journal

Much has been made recently of anti-French and anti-Quebec feeling in Western Canada, with Alberta being singled out by a Montreal roving newspaper reporter, in a series of articles, as the stronghold of such feelings.

I won't dispute his findings, knowing, as most reporters do, that if one searches long enough one will find whatever is being sought. Nor do I dispute the fact that such feelings exist, in Alberta as well as elsewhere in English-speaking Canada.

What I dispute is the image that particular series of articles tried to put across of an Alberta full of rednecked, cowboy-hatted bigots ready to fight the Plains of Abraham battle all over again. From my experience, and from very recent talks with many Franco-Albertans, that image is largely false.

In fact, French-Canadians here, particularly those born or grown up in Alberta, have done well over the years, have experienced little if any outright hostility or denial of any right, have not specifically been discriminated against – not any more than other minorities, in any case.

If anybody has encountered that kind of problem, it's Quebecers who came here recently, with the idea that they should be able to live a full daily life speaking exclusively in French, on account of the Official Languages Act. They quickly learned the futility of that dream, however, and developed a bitterness which, I am told by some Franco-Albertans, takes at least five years to disappear and, in some extreme cases, never really goes away.

The conclusion I have drawn, from talking to Franco-Albertans, is that the Official Languages Act and all the related federal push for bilingualism, rather than helping French-Canadians here, has created problems for them. It has transferred the French presence here from a well-established, well tolerated, largely cultural fact to a hot, resented political issue which has led to resistance or, to use a fashionable word, backlash.

Where politics comes in is in the equation by many Albertans of French-Canadianism with Liberalism and Trudeauism. It used to be a religious equation but now that has largely gone by the board and what has remained, according to Jocelyn Meunier, a former city nurse, is the belief that to have a French-Canadian name means being a Trudeau supporter. That is not necessarily true but it's believed to be true, and doesn't sit well with Albertans, she says.

Views of Franco-Albertans differ on details, but generally they agree life here hasn't been all that bad. Michel Meunier, now a Bonnyville lawyer after living in Edmonton and Calgary, has had a few unpleasant moments "but no rude encounters." Edmonton lawyer Louis Desrochers says "all is not perfect by any means" but has noticed "a growing acceptance of the French fact." As proof of that acceptance, Philippe Gibeau of Edmonton, a top provincial civil servant, points to the fact that he's had no problem being recently elected chairman of the city's separate school board.

"With a name like Gibeau I can't very well hide my origin," he explains, "and yet I've encountered little hostility. They voted for me. I know I have been accepted." As for Guy Pariseau, manager of French-language station CHFA, he admits he has "been rubbed the wrong way a few times" and told "to speak white," but he adds "it happens so seldom that it can be ignored as only the view of a few uneducated, ill-willed people."

Mr. Pariseau, on the other hand, has also been called a "traitor" in Quebec for his attachment to his native Alberta, and Mr. Meunier says that Quebecers generally lump Franco-Albertans under the label "Les assimiles." It means those who've been assimilated and is meant as an insult, though Franco-Albertans aren't bothered by it.

Of course there has been some assimilation, Mr. Pariseau admits. But he points to Quebec separatists wearing U.S. jeans or playing U.S. rock as just as assimilated, if that is the right word. Mr. Meunier also points out that Quebec is generous with descriptions such as that but never has given much else to French-Canadians here.

I get the impression there's little love lost between French-Canadians in Quebec and those outside Quebec. Franco-Albertans are proud of the fact they have been able to conserve their language and culture here without much help, from Ottawa or Quebec, and see that province's legislation, making French the official language in Quebec, as weakening the French language case elsewhere.

The French fact's record here is good. The Association Canadienne-Francaise de l'Alberta is 50 years old this year, for example, and CHFA, the Edmonton French station, is almost 30 years old. Life has not always been a bed of roses for those institutions, but they kept going when bilingualism and biculturalism were not yet words, let alone dirty words.

They are dirty, in the minds of some Albertans, not because of the principle invoked but because of the bungled federal application of it. Topping a bilingual federal sign in French, the bilingual can labels in the grocery store, that's what Mr. Desrochers calls "unnecessary provocation." Added to that there is the already-mentioned anti-Trudeau feeling in Alberta and, according to Mr. Meunier, the fact that "we used to be a cultural group – now we've become somewhat of a threat," almost like a fifth column.

He adds that if the federal and Quebec politicians "had left us alone and just encouraged French in the schools it would have been a damn good start." For him, and many other Franco-Albertans, language education in Alberta schools is essential. While it once was very difficult to get, it is now widely available, it's getting better, and it's much better used.

In the Edmonton separate school system alone, says Mr. Gibeau, of the 30,000 students everyone from Grade 4 on takes French, although a second language is not a requirement for graduation. Five schools have a purely bilingual program, funnelling students into bilingual high-school and, eventually, university. No backlash so far, he says, because the program "is voluntary and you can opt out." He does fear a backlash, however, and cries of "you're ramming French down my throat" if French is the only second language offered in the system. If it is, he says, it's because there are limited funds.

On the question of a Quebec separation, most Franco-Albertans would like to see Quebec stay in Confederation because they fear a break-up of Canada otherwise, and the loss of much beneficial input by that province, especially cultural. Most say the current English-French conflict is due to a lack of communication, due to a government stubbornly pushing a commitment while losing track of the reasons why a second language and culture is important.

"You can't pound that into people's heads through legislation," says Mr. Meunier. Mr. Gibeau sees the talk about separation as "a sign of strength on both sides," and he's happy for Quebec. However, if things continue as now "the price we would have to pay for unity would be outrageous," and a slowdown in the implementation of bilingualism programs is warranted. Canada "is still worth a compromise. We're much better as a nation from coast to coast," he says.

If some Albertans think that separation would rid them of the French-Canadians in their midst, I've got news for them. Most Franco-Albertans would stay right where they are – "I wouldn't know what to do in Quebec," says Mr. Pariseau – and that, I think, speaks better than anything else for the way Alberta has treated French-Canadians over the years. I think it's a tribute to both Francophones and Anglophones.

(f)
"An Enormous Myth..."

The Sault Star, *Sault Sainte Marie, Ontario, November 13, 1976*
Reprinted with permission of The Calgary Herald

THE CALGARY HERALD

We want a united Canada; a Canada that includes Quebec and which offers equality of opportunity to people of both French and English languages.

The Herald believes in that sort of Canada. Moreover, we believe that most Calgarians — and most Westerners — want such a Canada too, despite an enormous myth that is developing about the West's supposed hostility toward Quebec.

There is growing in this country, largely in Central Canada, a gigantic lie. It says that rejection of Quebec by the West is reaching proportions of hatred, racism, and worse.

It isn't true.

We believe the great majority of Westerners are moderate, open-minded, and good-willed in their perception of fellow Canadians everywhere, including French speaking Quebecers.

These reasonable views are being corrupted and debased in terms of perception elsewhere not by Westerners, but by a belief, fostered indirectly by Liberal politicians and adopted without examination by other citizens who ought to know better, that any breath of opposition to either the Liberal party or to its official bilingualism program is by definition racist.

That just simply isn't so.

The Trudeau administration has been despised in Western Canada for more than five years, not because of its bilingualism policies, but because it has provided astonishingly bad government. It has failed to comprehend, let alone face, some of the deep-seated Western anxieties about this region's own role in Confederation.

It has failed to provide even a modicum of sensible government for the nation as a whole.

In a more local sense this government has plundered Alberta's natural resources in a manner, had they tried even a fraction of it in Ontario or Quebec, would have led to the fall of the ministry within a few weeks of the attempt.

Now the most outlandish talk is rattling through the nation. So respected a senior journalist as Southam's own Charles Lynch tells a national television audience, during an interview with Joe Clark, that Canada may be "flying apart" and suggests that Western hostility is one of the main reasons.

Westerners have watched with growing incredulity the adoption by the national press corps of Bryce Mackasey as some sort of contemporary folk hero after his unexplained and, to Westerners, unlamented departure from the federal cabinet.

This theatrical politician, whose main contribution to public life was the creation of an Unemployment Insurance Act that later had to be substantially amended by his own colleagues, is now slavishly quoted even when he comes out with such dangerous nonsense as comparing Canada today with Northern Ireland.

(This idea is spreading. The president of the Canadian Council of Christians and Jews, Dr. Peter Jones of Toronto, said in Calgary just the other day that Westerners' increasing hostility towards French Canadians verges on racism of the type suffered in the past by Jews. This we reject absolutely. It dishonors and renders ludicrous a distinguished organization.)

Further evidence of Western enmity is being found in the James Richardson case. For reasons apparently having to do with entrenchment of language rights in the constitution — reasons that were politically incomprehensible and intellectually indigestible, this man, too, left the cabinet. Whatever role Mr. Richardson plays in Winnipeg's scheme of things, he is not a leader of Western Canadians generally. He never has been.

It is important to restate a Western view, and to refute some of these dismal propositions at this time, because the growing mythology has implications broader than just a general smear of Western Canadians. It suggests that the national Conservative party under Alberta's Joe Clark cannot, by definition, lead this divided country. That merely panders to the Liberal notion that they, and they alone, are fit to govern.

Make no mistake about it. Lots of Westerners regard aspects of the bilingualism policy with disfavor — not so much because those aspects are sinister but because they are silly. The packaging and labelling regulations, in combination with the grim dictate that the dismal chemicals that comprise so much of modern food be listed, produces a two-tongue clutter in this region to the general benefit of no one.

This expensive attempt to educate civil servants in a second language was known to be a failure in Western Canada long before the government acknowledged it, because many sons or daughters of the West were involved.

Westerners argued for years that the way to approach language was through the schools. Despite a lack of federal support so complete that only in this past month has the government even acknowledged it, that is exactly what has been happening in Alberta. Thousands of people flock to French courses where once only hundreds or scores did. Bilingual schools are flourishing. With adequate federal aid it might be possible to multiply these efforts. As it is, they stand in mute testimony to a love of Canada.

Instead of learning about these things and seeking to assist them, the new secretary of state for Canada sits in Toronto and gives interviews including the hoary old yarn about the Westerner who supposedly believed that a Mountie would one day tell him that he must learn French. This man, one John Roberts, augurs well to fittingly succeed Hugh Faulkner as a promoter of narrow nationalism that is as repugnant to Western Canadians as it is to Quebecers because it seeks to bottle all Canadians up in our own juices and insulate our tender minds from people in other countries.

There are a lot of perfectly legitimate points of

discussion surrounding Quebec's relationship with the other nine provinces. There always have been. There always will be. We know that in Alberta with particular force, because many of Robert Bourassa's positions are also Peter Lougheed's positions.

The two governments have a relationship that is among the closest of any pair of governments in this too-often squabbling nation. That relationship is perfectly well-known to Lougheed's voters. They don't abuse him for it.

One constant Western preoccupation is with transportation of people and goods. It is surely self-evident that mutual understanding at the people-to-people level would be greatly enhanced in this vast country by the provision of cheap and easy travel. Instead this Liberal government doggedly espouses a user-pays transportation formula which mitigates most strongly against those in the extremities of the nation. They have increased the obstacles to travel, not decreased them.

Let's face one thing squarely. There are bigots in Western Canada. But we say that there are no more proportionately than in any other part of the country. There are people who would be prepared to see Quebec leave Confederation. But we would say there are no more of them (and in fact are likely less of them) than in Ontario.

This newspaper believes in a united Canada of which Quebec is an integral part, and within which the preservation of French language and culture and opportunity is an explicit national goal.

We remain free to argue the means to that end as we always have. Calgarians and Westerners generally are not racists, they are not separatists, and they are sickened by references to Northern Ireland.

It is not from Westerners that those allusions come.

* * *

II. ONTARIO

(a)

Francophones Find Few Ontario Services

The Toronto Star, *April 16, 1977*
Reprinted with permission – The Toronto Star

By Elaine Carey
Star staff writer

Thirty-five per cent of the patients at the Brockville Psychiatric Hospital are French-speaking, but if they want to be treated, they have to learn English first.

There, and in other hospitals in the province, "the atmosphere is so culturally and linguistically English that a patient must virtually forget his language, his culture, in order to adapt himself to the surroundings. Some of the patients are able to do so but will never be able to relate again to their families."

That example comes from a 255-page provincial government task force report, released last October, which concludes the province's health ministry displays "a total lack of concern for anything connected with French language and culture" in any of its services for the sick, mentally ill and handicapped.

* * *

Ontario's new health minister, Dennis Timbrell, said in an interview that since taking over the health ministry last month, he has set his staff to work on the task force report and some government statement on it should be forthcoming by the end of April.

* * *

In the words of Giselle Richer, president of l'Association Canadienne Francaise de l'Ontario, health services are the most vital area of concern for Francophones because "It's not an area where anyone has any choice over what they can do. You do not choose to be sick."

* * *

Since then, the government has quietly built

French-language schools, issued drivers' licenses and other documents in both languages, and established an experimental bilingual court in Sudbury.

* * *

In Essex County, where there are 50,000 Francophones, the French-language action committee has been struggling for eight years to get a French-language high school for Windsor-area children.

Two years ago, the trustees of the Essex County Board of Education voted in favor of building it but changed their minds a year later when the province lowered its capital grants for new schools as a restraint measure.

In the past year, feelings about the issue have run so high and gained such national attention that even when education minister Wells announced the province would pay more than 95 per cent of the cost of the school, the trustees voted against it.

Now Wells has introduced legislation to force the trustees to build the school but in Essex it may take more than legislation to cool out hostilities between the English and French.

The struggle for the high school has even gained prominent attention in Quebec papers as an example of how little the rest of the country cares about the French.

The government appears to be moving quickly to make sure issues like Essex County don't crop up again.

* * *

The province now has 24 French-language secondary schools with an enrolment of 31,392 students and 59 others with some French-language classes. In addition, there are 303 public and separate elementary schools with all or some classes in French.

* * *

In 1974, the ministerial committee on the teaching of French recommended to Wells that Ontario schools begin teaching French in kindergarten and that by Grade 6, every student have studied it for an accumulated total of 180 minutes a day. Grades 7 and 8 students should study French for three hours and 20 minutes a week.

"It is the basic right of every child to learn French by the best available methods for as many school years as he can profit from the experience," the report said.

(b)

Filion Affair Called Disgrace to Ontario

The Toronto Star, *July 16, 1977*
Reprinted with permission – The Toronto Star

By Robert McKenzie
Star staff writer

QUEBEC

The case of Gerard Filion, the former newspaper publisher whose well-publicized attempts to obtain a French trial in Ontario have so far failed, is proving an acute embarrassment to defenders of English minority rights in Quebec.

* * *

Filion, who will be 68 next month, is one of 19 people facing charges of conspiracy to rig dredging-contract bids in 1969 and 1971 when he was president of a Quebec-based company, Marine Industries Ltd.

After being ordered last December to stand trial, Filion wrote McMurtry pleading for a separate trial in French.

He argued that he would be at a disadvantage before an English-speaking judge and jury. The alleged offences relate to dredging contracts at Beauport and Ile d'Orleans near Quebec City while several of the other defendants are linked with alleged offences in Hamilton.

* * *

"I am a French-speaking Canadian citizen

resident in the province of Quebec," he wrote. "The illegal acts of which I am accused are supposed to have been committed against the government of Canada. It is a federal organization, the Royal Canadian Mounted Police, which laid the charge against me.

"As a Canadian citizen, accused by the government of my country, I am seeking the right to be judged in French by a court composed of a French-speaking judge and 12 French-speaking members of a jury.

"I refuse to admit that there could be two categories of citizens in this country: A first-class category, English-speaking, having the right to be judged by their peers in the 10 Canadian provinces and a category of second-class citizens, French-speaking, who are refused this fundamental right outside the frontiers of the Quebec reserve."

McMurtry's reply on May 2 touched off a controversy which has been growing ever since in Quebec. He said he could not accept that it was second-class justice to have an English-speaking judge and jury in Ontario — any more than an English-speaking resident of Ontario would have anything to fear before a French-speaking judge and jury in Quebec.

Filion replied on May 22: "The situation you describe to back up your reasoning could never happen because, for the last 110 years, Quebec has had English-language civil and criminal courts to handle court procedures in English.

"Your English-speaking businessman from Ontario would be judged in Quebec by an English-speaking judge and jury and all the procedures would be in English."

* * *

The greatest danger in the Filion affair, it [*Le Devoir*] said, is that "without wishing to do so, (the Ontario government) will have convinced thousands of citizens of this country that Canadian justice speaks a different language when you move from one province to another."

Filion's own lawyer, Jacques Bellemare, a former dean of the University of Montreal law faculty, recalled that during his client's preliminary inquiry in Toronto, hockey fans at Maple Leaf Gardens booed the singing of O Canada in French.

(c)

Letter to the Editor

The Globe and Mail, *Toronto*
November 11, 1976
Reprinted with permission of the writer

As a Franco-Ontarian, I do not expect that all Ontarians speak French. I think, though, that I am at least entitled to respect for my mother tongue in Ontario.

An understanding and appreciation of the language and culture of the two founding races of this country is one of the corner-stones of Confederation. Vincent Massey, in his opening remarks on the Royal Commission of Inquiry into Culture, once stated: "Let me say, quite frankly and humbly, that it has taken us in English-speaking Canada a long time to realize that there are two cultures in this country and that our French-speaking fellow citizens were here before us. It must be remembered that more than a quarter of our population comes of neither French nor British stock. We welcome the cultures which these people have brought with them; we value the rich contribution they make to our national life. We, however, have two founding races, French and English in origin; their languages and cultures having a special and permanent place in the national scene. This is an historical fact, not a political judgment."

I do hope that the younger generation will develop a sentiment of tolerance and respect for people which has been a characteristic of this province and of Canada. Before embarking on bilingual programs in the schools, it would be wise to impart a greater emphasis on Canadian history to our children.

Omer Deslauriers, Chairman
Advisory Council for
Franco-Ontarian Affairs
Toronto

(d)
Davis Kills Language Bill Hopes

The Sault Star, *Sault Sainte Marie,
Ontario, June 2, 1978
Reprinted with permission of The
Canadian Press*

TORONTO (CP) — Any hope that a private member's bill calling for French language services in Ontario might become law has been dashed by Premier William Davis.

The bill, calling for educational, judicial, health, social, municipal and other services in French, received second reading in the legislature Thursday and was supported in principle by all parties.

The bill, introduced by Albert Roy (L—Ottawa East), was sent to the justice committee for clause-by-clause study, usually a prelude to third reading and final approval.

However, Premier Davis issued a statement shortly after several members of his cabinet had spoken in favor of the bill, saying it would not proceed through third reading.

"I regard today's vote as an endorsement of our position," the premier said in his statement. "The government will proceed no further with the private bill. Neither shall we be taking any steps to declare French an official language in Ontario."

He said his decision was based on the conviction that the government already has in place a course of action consistent with the sentiments of the people of Ontario and the needs of the province's francophone citizens.

Michael Cassidy, leader of the New Democrats, rose in the house when the legislature resumed sitting in the evening and called for the house to adjourn in protest over the premier's statement.

Cassidy said it was a deliberate deception and an arrogant disregard of the legislature.

Liberal Leader Stuart Smith, who was generous in his praise of the Conservatives for allowing a free vote on Roy's bill, said later he was not entirely surprised that the premier would allow the bill to die on the order paper but was disappointed with the government's action.

In the legislature, Smith said the bill removes the language issue from the political realm and gives franco-Ontarians the feeling their rights are being enshrined in law.

"The bill itself doesn't go as far as some would like, but it goes, I think, as far as it should at this time."

The large majority of the members were in the house for the voice vote on Roy's bill, but a number of members did not return after the dinner break.

In the evening session, the division bells rang for an hour calling members back to the house. Then the Liberals joined the Conservatives to defeat Cassidy's motion to adjourn by a vote of 54 to 26 and the house continued its business.

Jim Breithaupt (L — Kitchener) said the Liberals supported the government because the premier's statement was in order even though it was not prudent.

He said the bill still can proceed through committee, a majority of whose members belong to the opposition parties.

The bill was introduced under new rules of the legislature, which set aside one day a week for private member's bills.

The government, which could have blocked second reading by having at least 20 of its members stand in opposition to the bill, allowed a free vote with each MPP voting as an individual instead of along party lines.

Outside the legislature, the premier denied he had killed the bill. He said it had been tradition that private members' bills would be introduced for debate and sometimes carried beyond first and second reading, but that it would be leading people astray to say such a bill could be carried through to its conclusion.

The bill passed second reading on a voice vote with no dissenting voices heard.

However, spokesmen from Liberal and Conservative parties said outside the house that a recorded vote would not have been unanimous.

It takes five members to force a formal count but one was not requested.

In speaking to his bill, Roy said there was no intention to shove French down anyone's throat.

"It is to legislate the rights of franco-Ontarians as the rights of others are legislated — no more, no less."

He said the strategy of the Parti Quebecois was to annoy and intimidate the rest of Canada until people outside Quebec finally said: "Let 'em go for God's sake."

He said his bill would send a strong message to

Quebecers' saying the people of Ontario care about them.

The bill would establish the office of a French language services co-ordinator and a language service board to help improve the availability of French language services.

Roy praised the government for steps it already has taken in providing French services, particularly in the courts.

Cassidy while supporting the bill in principle, called it weak and said it did not go far enough. "It's a step in the right direction, however."

He expressed concern that if it were made law it would prove ineffectual because the civil service might not carry out the commitment of the bill.

Rene Brunelle, provincial secretary for resources development, was the first government speaker and said it had always been the government's approach not to enforce anything on anyone.

He said the position of the government was to recognize the fundamental right of an education in French. The government, he said, was proud of its course of action and was not altering its policies by supporting the bill.

Education Minister Thomas Wells also spoke in favor of the bill saying he was particularly proud of what Ontario has done in French education.

Wells said he would like to believe there is not one member of the legislature who would not basically agree with the principle of the bill.

Gordon Walker (PC—London South) issued a statement saying he opposed the bill.

He called it a bureaucratic nightmare which would cause new mazes of red tape and be costly to administer.

III. ANGLOPHONE QUEBEC

Letter to the Editor

The Montreal Star, *August 20, 1977*
Reprinted with permission of the writer

Sir, — With reference to recent reports of people of French culture living in other provinces (British Columbia), and who feel they are being denied a fair shake with regards to education, advertising, shopping facilities etc. etc.

I am left speechless. Surely there is a lack of common sense in their attitude and demands? Are they afraid they are going to lose their identity and French culture? Damned ridiculous, I say.

I am a Scot, having lived in La Belle Province for 47 years. I have absolutely no fear of losing my identity or culture, but the longer I live here the more I am convinced that a large number of its inhabitants are simply crazy.

Nobody, but nobody, can tell anyone what language they are going to speak or what type of education their children are going to receive. English, French, German, Italian, Greek, Polish, Hungarian, Spanish, Chinese, Japanese and a hundred more — they are all good. To learn one more language is knowledge. When will we ever learn that out of a thousand volumes comes one page of wisdom? It is not a matter of what language one speaks, but how one says it.

The more so-called "progress" Mr. Lévesque and his government makes the more they should realize what a futile and unrewarding journey it is. Politics, religion, press and labor must surely be interdependent on one another? Understanding, compassion, honesty, sincerity, faith, hope and charity are all ingredients of the pudding. Find the ones that are missing and perhaps we are all on the road to a better society, a much tastier pudding and a happier people.

James M. D. Babington,
Ste. Thérèse de Blainville.

IV. EASTERN CANADA

(a) NEW BRUNSWICK

The Globe and Mail, *Toronto, August 20, 1977*

English Dominates New Brunswick Despite Established French Presence

Provincial services in New Brunswick are provided in both English and French, since New Brunswick proclaimed itself to have two official languages in 1969. (Parts of the law were proclaimed later, the last on July 1 of this year.)

Education, considered a provincial service, is generally provided in either English or French, but there are areas in the province where the Acadians are in a minority with no French education yet available.

In the largest city, Saint John, there are 6,925 people whose mother tongue is French. But there were no French classes for them until this past year, and then only Grade One was made available. This fall, a second grade will be added, and in a few years there will be a French elementary school.

In several other places in the province there are French classes, but they are within a school that has an English-speaking administration and other classes which are taught in English.

Some change is slowly coming to the English-language areas of New Brunswick. But a person going to Moncton and making a few inquiries in French rapidly discovers that French is not generally considered an official language.

* * *

The New Brunswick Ministry of Tourism announced a few days ago that more tourists came from Quebec this summer than anywhere else, and that Quebec tourists stayed 20 per cent longer than other tourists.

Yet the reporter called to the Moncton tourist bureau and asked, in French, if he could be given tourist information in French.

The answer was no.

He asked if there was anyone there who understood French.

The answer, again, was no.

* * *

Bathurst is a city of 16,675 people, according to the 1971 census, and 52 per cent of the population then had French as their mother tongue. More French people have moved in since, according to reports. It is the service centre of Gloucester County, which is 83 per cent French. Most of the signs in the commercial establishments of Bathurst are in English only. The local movie theatre shows films in English. Proceedings of the city council are in English. But people wanting municipal services can get them in English or French, even though not all municipal employees can speak French.

In the predominantly English-speaking parts of the province, services in French at the municipal level or in establishments dealing with the public are usually non-existent.

The capital city of the province, Fredericton, remains an English city. Municipal services "are all in one language," English, according to Mayor Elbridge Wilkins. "We've always been a predominantly English-speaking city."

Fredericton, a city of 24,255 in 1971, has 2,070 people of French origin, but French is the mother tongue of only 1,450 of them. The others have lost the language.

* * *

In Acadian counties, French is spoken largely by the French when they are among themselves, but English is the usual language used in exchanges between people of French and non-French origin. This, however, is beginning to change, with some Acadians insisting on speaking French. This causes indignation among the others...

The largest local employer [in Edmundston], Fraser Companies Ltd., is a pulp mill with "close to 1,000 employees," according to

Lawrence Fyfe, manager of public relations for the company. The working language of the company is English, according to Mr. Fyfe.

Of the 18 most senior officials of the company listed in the Edmundston phone book, only one is of French mother tongue. Until recent years, according to Mr. Tweedie, the company was unfavorably disposed to hiring people of French origin.

"They wouldn't appoint a Catholic, even, to a responsible position. Certainly not a Frenchman. That's a well-known fact — Fraser was no place for a Frenchman."

* * *

(b) NOVA SCOTIA

The Globe and Mail, *Toronto, July 5, 1976*

Nova Scotia: "I Get Upset at People Trying To Push It On You"

By Thomas Coleman
Globe and Mail Reporter

KENTVILLE, N.S. — Mention bilingualism on Main Street in the Nova Scotia heartland and the reply starts to sound like a broken record. "We don't like having anything shoved down our throats like they're trying to do with French..."

In the Annapolis Valley, where more than 98 per cent of the residents come from English-speaking stock, there is not only very little sympathy for French-Canadian aspirations, there is outright resentment, in many cases, of the gains Francophones have made in recent years within Confederation.

Of more than 34 people questioned in the farming towns of Kentville, New Minas and Wolfville, only five expressed any real sympathy for the language rights of French Canadians. For many, bilingualism meant Quebec rather than French Canadian and two suggested bilingualism could lead to armed conflict within Canada....

(c) NEWFOUNDLAND

The Globe and Mail, *Toronto,*
November 11, 1976

French in Newfoundland Gets New Life

By Marie Gleason
Special to The Globe and Mail

CAPE ST. GEORGE, Nfld. — "Henri, come on, get up now; you promised to review your French before school this morning."

With a total absence of the resistance one might reasonably expect from 13-year-old boys roused from their warm beds to study French nouns they take out their cahiers and recite aloud to one another.

* * *

The Simon family is of French origin, but for Josephine and the two boys, English is their mother tongue; Henri Sr. is bilingual. In spite of the considerable Anglicization of Cape shore residents in the past 30 years, Henri Sr. and a good many others like him managed to retain spoken fluency in their native French.

It's not too late for Henri Sr.'s generation to read and write French either; a course for adults is being offered in Cape schools. In this remote and starkly beautiful peninsula, encapsulated in the anglophone society of Newfoundland, native francophones are rediscovering their heritage. In the rush of change, boys the age of Henri and Alex seem willing, even eager, to learn French.

* * *

During the 18th and 19th centuries, French fishermen came from St. Pierre and Miquelon, continental France and the Magdalen Islands. A few jumped ship to escape the hardships of life aboard the fishing vessels of the day. Because of English-French treaties, they had fishing, if not settlers' rights.

In 1904, what was called the French Shore came under Newfoundland's jurisdiction. Still, because of its isolation, the fisherman-woodsman-farmer subsistence economy, particularly in the Cape area, remained largely francophone.

During the Second World War, a U.S. airbase in Stephenville drew both francophones and Newfoundland anglophones into its economic orbit and cash economy. That, plus English-language schooling, contributed to the erosion of the French culture and language.

With increased federal emphasis and support of bilingualism, the trend appears to have been arrested. Two organizations, Terreneuviens francais, a local group organized in 1971 and the Port-au-Port Roman Catholic school board, have been instrumental in the changes.

V. SUMMARY

The Sault Star, *Sault Sainte Marie, Ontario, April 1, 1977*
Reprinted with permission of
The Canadian Press

Most Provinces Want English as Main Language

By the Canadian Press

The language rights of French speaking Canadians vary from province to province, but a Cross-Canada survey by The Canadian Press shows that most provincial governments seem content to retain English as the main language.

Federally, the Official Languages Act provides general guarantees of service to French citizens in their own language, wherever possible.

Under the act, the government may designate an area as bilingual when French- and English-speaking residents make up at least 10 per cent of the area's total population.

The following is a regional summary of the legal rights extended by provinces to the French language.

Atlantic provinces — There is no legislation in Newfoundland requiring that French be used for any purpose. French is not a compulsory subject in schools, although it is taught in most.

In Prince Edward Island, French-language instruction is compulsory in Grades 7 to 9 with any other requirements left to the discretion of local school boards. Currently, about 80 per cent of P.E.I. schoolchildren in Grades 4 to 9 take French.

There are no compulsory French courses in primary or secondary schools in Nova Scotia although the ministry of education said recently it would like to introduce French if needed funds are made available.

The last sections of New Brunswick's Official Languages Act, passed in [1969], come into effect July 1 and require all government departments to provide services to the public in both official languages.

Ontario — The Ontario government plans to improve services to francophones in their language. French is not compulsory in any English-language schools, but the province encourages school boards to teach French through a grant system partly supported by the federal government.

The official language in Ontario's court system is English although steps are being taken to offer provincial court services in French, especially since 21 persons went to jail rather than pay fines to protest unilingual traffic or parking summonses. Drivers' licences now are being issued in both languages and most ordinary court documents are also available in French.

There are no regulations in the province requiring private businesses to provide any services in French.

The Prairies — French-language instruction in Manitoba is not compulsory in any grades although some school boards do offer French courses. Court proceedings, legal documents and private business dealings are carried out in English.

In Saskatchewan, a second language is required in Grades 7 to 9, but it does not have to be French.

In Alberta, French is not compulsory in schools and no regulations exist making the use of French in government departments or private business necessary.

* * *

NEW HOPE FOR FRENCH-CANADIAN SURVIVAL OUTSIDE QUEBEC

Developments in 1978 gave promise of some reversal of this trend to assimilation with the agreement of the ten provincial premiers at a Conference in Montreal which recognized the right of francophone and anglophone Canadians to an education in the language of their ethnic origin in all of Canada's ten provinces. While the premiers left it to each province to determine how this principle was to be implemented, this was the first time in Canadian history that such a declaration of policy, recognizing the right of French Canadians outside Quebec to a French-language education, had been made by the ten provinces as a collectivity.

How fast and to what extent this new policy would be put into practice remained for the future to determine, but it gave promise of a possible reversal of the loss of language fluency by French Canadians outside Quebec.

A new organization of French Canadians outside Quebec — the Fédération des Francophones Hors Québec — was voicing the new determination of their constituency to put into practice the principle enunciated in Montreal in February 1978 by the ten premiers.

The Task Force on Canadian Unity noted this growth in concern for the situation of French Canadians outside Quebec:

> At the provincial level, increased recognition has also been given to the needs of the French Canadians, especially in the provinces of New Brunswick and Ontario, where the majority of the French-speaking population outside Quebec live. With an Acadian minority representing a third of its total population, New Brunswick wisely accepted the B&B Commission's invitation to declare itself officially bilingual and has begun the slow process of adapting the structure and services of the province to this linguistic reality. Ontario, on the other hand, with only 5.6 per cent of its population French-speaking, did not accept the recommendations of the commission but has continued the development of French-language services on which it was already embarked. The seriousness of the effort that Ontario has made, for instance, in the field of education, can be glimpsed from the Council of Ministers of Education's estimate that 93.6 per cent of potential French-language students in Ontario are now enrolled in French-language programs at the elementary and secondary levels.
>
> – The Task Force on Canadian Unity, *A Future Together: Observations and Recommendations* (Ottawa: January, 1979), pp.12–13

The extracts which follow illustrate the vigor with which many French Canadians outside Quebec are pursuing the demand for recognition of the right to secure the provisions of schools in which French is the language of communication and instruction. The extract from the First Report of the Ontario Advisory Committee on Confederation indicates increased awareness on Ontario's part of Franco-Ontarian needs.

The extent to which realization of this demand is influenced by Quebec's status within the Canadian confederation is difficult to determine. It is clear, however, that the one and a half million French Canadians outside Quebec are more determined today than at any time in the past one hundred years to retain the culture of their ancestors.

The Toronto Star, *February 24, 1978*
Reprinted with permission
- The Toronto Star

Quebec Backs Language Rights

By Chrys Goyens
Star staff writer

MONTREAL — The premiers of Canada's nine English provinces have achieved what they could not last August in St. Andrews, N.B. by getting Quebec to go along with a general statement of principle dealing with minority language rights in Canada.

The statement of principle, which emerged from a meeting of premiers here yesterday, is that each child of a French-speaking minority (or in Quebec, the English-speaking minority) is entitled to an education in his or her language in primary or secondary schools in each province — where numbers warrant.

That is no change from the document which Quebec refused to sign at the New Brunswick seaside resort last summer. However, Quebec relented yesterday when another principle was added to the official statement which read:

"It is understood, due to exclusive jurisdiction of provincial governments in the field of education, and due also to wide cultural and demographic differences, that the implementation of the foregoing principle would be as defined by each province."

Many observers here believe that this public reaffirmation of provincial jurisdiction in education provided the concessions which Quebec sought.

Apart from the statement of principle, the premiers did not take it upon themselves to make any formal commitments.

The Globe and Mail, *Toronto, June 23, 1977*
Reprinted with permission of The Canadian Press

Bilingual Schools Threaten Assimilation of Francophones, Group Says

OTTAWA (CP) — Bilingual schools are one of the strongest forces for assimilating French Canadians into the English-speaking community, a group representing French-Canadian youth outside Quebec said yesterday.

Instead of helping French-Canadian young people preserve their language, the constant interaction with English-Canadian students results in their assimilation, said a report released by the Federation des Jeunes Canadiens-Francais.

Even when a majority of classes is given in French, English-speaking students insure that English is the dominant language in the hallways and playground, said the federation, which is composed of French-Canadian youth groups in the nine English-speaking provinces.

The group warned that there could be violence.

"Is it necessary to recall that in South Africa bombs exploded because of color and in Ireland for religion? Will it soon be our turn because of culture or language?"

The federation described bilingual schools as "arsenic administered to the human body in weak doses." Unless a unilingual French school system were established for French communities across Canada, the French-Canadian culture outside Quebec would vanish.

"When you have two languages, it is evident that one has to go," Gilles Dureault, Manitoba's representative, said at a news conference.

Jacques Laprise, president of the Ottawa-based federation, said unless the Government intervenes, within five years French-Canadian youth outside Quebec will be almost completely assimilated.

Beside the establishment of unilingual French schools, the federation wanted more funds from the federal Government to establish YMCA-like recreational institutions for French Canadians.

The group's aims are similar to those of the Federation des Francophones Hors Quebec, the largest voice for the one million French Canadians outside Quebec. After intense lobbying by this organization, Prime Minister Pierre Trudeau announced formation of an interdepartmental study to investigate its allegations that assimilation continues.

Secretary of State John Roberts tabled a language policy paper in the Commons on Tuesday that urges the provinces to improve services to their French-speaking minorities, especially by providing more schools.

* * *

The Sault Star, *Sault Sainte Marie, Ontario, April 5, 1978*

Francophones Protest Denial of Twin School

By Catharine Dixon
Of the Star

BLIND RIVER — Approximately 40 members of the francophone community attended a meeting of the North Shore Board of Education (NSBE) Monday evening to protest the board's decision not to comply with a request by the French Language Advisory Committee (FLAC) to establish a twin school for francophones at the W. C. Eaket secondary school here.

Jean Senechal, FLAC chairman, also presented a petition containing 175 signatures in support of a twin school for francophones to operate in a similar fashion to Villa Franco-Jeunesse in Elliot Lake.

Villa Franco-Jeunesse, with an enrolment of slightly more than 200 French-speaking students, is situated in portable classrooms attached to the Elliot Lake secondary school (ELSS) with which it shares several facilities such as the cafeteria and library.

In the case of the W. C. Eaket school, there would be room within the confines of the present building to house both an English-speaking and French-speaking secondary school.

A wing for francophone students has already been established there but FLAC would like this wing to have its own name, its own public address system, its own guidance services and its own principal. In effect, to be an autonomous school having equal status with its English counterpart.

In rejecting FLAC's request, the board wrote that a majority of trustees felt more public input was required before setting up a twin school according to the FLAC recommendation.

Mr. Senechal reminded trustees that FLAC was a duly elected body representing francophone ratepayers within the jurisdiction of the board and "as such, has adequately surveyed the francophone population on this issue as supported by some 175 signatures."

The NSBE told FLAC in its letter of refusal that, "it was also a majority feeling that the present French wing provided the French-speaking students with the most viable organization in view of the need to share program and facilities with the English section under the over-all jurisdiction of one principal."

"The committee would like to reiterate its stand that the only organization that will meet the needs of our francophone students is an autonomous unit, in this case a twin school," said Mr. Senechal.

The board said further that the full financial impact of establishing a twin school as requested could not be determined without a great deal more study.

Mr. Senechal pointed out that the FLAC recommendation had originally been submitted in June, 1977 and that the committee granted a further extension at the board's request until March 15 for an answer.

"The members of FLAC deplore the fact that the board could not submit a full financial reasoning," said Mr. Senechal.

Mr. Senechal noted further that the board had turned down a motion approving the FLAC recommendations in principle, but that in a subsequent motion it had "recognized the principle of the FLAC recommendations."

"What distinction do you make between approving in principle in your first motion which was defeated and recognizing in principle which was approved in your second motion?" asked Mr. Senechal.

At a meeting of FLAC on April 10, the committee will consider what action is to be taken following the board's refusal to implement its recommendations, Mr. Senechal mentioned.

One of the crowd of FLAC supporters present, Pierrette Menard, asked Board members to try to put themselves into the shoes of the minority francophone group.

"How would you like to see your children of English descent assimilated very quickly by French Canadians?" she asked.

"I'm sure you would feel it your duty to act to stop this genocide of the anglo culture," she told the board.

"If this right of free expression in one's culture, so highly recommended by both levels of government, were denied, how would you feel?" she asked.

Mrs. Menard said she was proud to be able to speak fluently in both English and French because she had been educated at St. Joseph's French-speaking private high school in Blind River, she maintained that such fluency as she possessed in both tongues would not be possible for children educated in a high shool "with the system that exists at W. C. Eaket."

She received a hearty round of applause.

Clarence Eaket, board chairman, said he felt that students would not be able to get sufficient options if separate schools for English and French were established, but a French-speaking parent said they would be happier to have fewer options in French.

"The basics are essential for the French student," she said. "They're not really interested in a lot of options which they don't really want."

Mrs. Lucille Laderoute pointed out that a five-year study had indicated there were sufficient students to offer the required courses.

"Whatever happened to that study?" she asked.

Board vice-chairman Robert Whitehead said he couldn't see how two bosses (principals) could operate in one school.

He said there couldn't be two masters in one house. That would be like putting two women in one kitchen, he said.

Trustee Marcel Bruneau pointed out that Villa Franco-Jeunesse and Elliot Lake secondary school got along well under one roof with two principals and couldn't see why this same system couldn't work in Blind River.

* * *

The Globe and Mail, *Toronto, October 28, 1976*

Alberta's French fear language doomed
Unilingual schools way to bilingualism?

By Mary Kate Rowan
Special to The Globe and Mail

EDMONTON — One of every three French Canadians in Alberta has forgotten how to speak French, says Herve Durocher, president of the 10,000 member Association Canadienne-Française de l'Alberta.

Mr. Durocher, a lawyer, recommended that Alberta establish unilingual French public schools "geared to slowing down, stopping and reversing" the weakening of French culture in Alberta.

"Bilingual schools are not good enough,"

Mr. Durocher said in an interview.

He said that Franco-Albertans make up 2 per cent of the population in Alberta and 5 per cent in Edmonton.

Children who attend bilingual schools receive half their education in French. However, Mr. Durocher said, because the French community is small, most French children speak English most of the time when they are not at school because the majority of their playmates are English.

As a result, Mr. Durocher said, by the time French children end Grade 6 in a bilingual school, they are more proficient in English than in French.

He said that in Alberta "bilingual schools don't create a bilingual (Franco-Albertan) child. To create a bilingual child you need a unilingual school."

He said that the English influence in Alberta is so strong that French children would learn to speak perfect English even if their public school held all classes in French. "Our children are going to learn English whether we like it or not," he said. He used his own family as an example.

He and his wife speak French at home. His oldest child, a 6-year-old girl, who went to a French day-care centre, is perfectly bilingual. She had to learn English to play with her friends, who are all English. Her 3½-year-old brother understands French but, when given a choice, prefers to speak English.

"Because he's a second child he learns how to speak from his sister and not so much from his sister speaking to us in French but from his sister speaking with her playmates in English.

"That brings me and that brings many parents like me to the point where we say here in Alberta that we have bilingual schools where it is permitted to teach our children 50 per cent in French and 50 per cent by law in English. We say who needs it?

"I think when you reach Grade 7, Grade 8, Grade 9 where you start to learn the intricacies of a language you need some instruction (in English) but before that the children will learn English very, very easily."

Mr. Durocher says his feelings are shared by "the teachers in the bilingual schools and the parents of young French-Canadian children."

That statement will be tested the first weekend in November when Alberta's French-Canadian association will hold a conference to celebrate its 50th anniversary.

The conference will take a firm position on unilingual French schools. He does say, though, that if it does he won't be the least bit surprised.

The Globe and Mail,
Toronto, August 13, 1977

One-Language Education Best Bet for Franco-Ontarians

By Yves Lavigne

Franco-Ontarian students attending Grades 12 and 13 in French-language high schools are more confident, ambitious, and more likely to succeed in white-collar jobs than their counterparts in mixed language high schools, concludes a Government report.

"It is difficult to be part of a minority group, when one must live one's life in the midst of a majority speaking another language, but, when one undertakes studies in an institution serving exclusively the linguistic minority, one is sheltered from ill feelings associated with being part of a minority," the report says.

"Francophone students enrolled in mixed high schools seem to express less desire to pursue a university career... they seem to have a lower self-evaluation."

More Franco-Ontarians in the Kent-Essex Windsor-Lambton area attend mixed high schools than in any other part of the province. Eighty-one per cent of the Grades 12 and 13 Franco-Ontarian students do so because they have no choice, the report says. For many, there are no French-language high schools for them to go to.

In the Ottawa-Carleton area, 90 per cent of Franco-Ontarian students attend French-language high schools.

The situation in the Windsor area is bound to change, however, since a recent legislative act ordered the construction of a French high school in Essex County.

The report, completed more than a year ago, was intended for Government policy making and was not widely distributed. It was commissioned by the province's Advisory Council for Franco-

Ontarian Affairs and paid for by the Ministry of Colleges and Universities.

A total of 4,517 students — 70 per cent of the Grades 12 and 13 Franco-Ontarian students in the province — were polled.

The type of high school was judged to be the most important factor influencing the choice of life goals by Franco-Ontarians. That, however, was not the only factor. Others involved sex, socio-economic status, how many languages parents know, and competence in English.

The report says that females, although more successful in primary grades, don't show the interest that males show in a university education.

It says students with unilingual parents underestimate their scholastic aptitudes, as do those from working-class families and that poor knowledge of English leads to a lowering of self-confidence.

The report notes that most students intent on getting a university education want a bilingual education in a bilingual institution.

The 66 per cent who want this show a marked tendency to gravitate towards bilingual cities. Of those who attend universities, 57 per cent have chosen the University of Ottawa. Algonquin College in Ottawa attracts 47 per cent of the students who want a technologically geared education.

This kind of concentration of services for francophones could render other institutions less inclined to offer more services in French, the report says. This could create disadvantages for students who want to study in other parts of the province.

The report concludes that "it is important that Franco-Ontarian students not become handicapped in their educational, vocational and professional choices because of their mother tongue."

It also asks that colleges and universities provide more services for Franco-Ontarians.

FIRST REPORT OF THE ONTARIO ADVISORY COMMITTEE ON CONFEDERATION, APRIL 1978

V. Language Rights

GENERAL
- The Committee has scrutinized the programs of the Ontario government that provide French language services to the Franco-Ontarian community in an increasing number of fields, e.g., education, courts, health, social services, transportation, official publications. It recognizes further steps should be taken perhaps along the lines of a French language services act supporting French language guarantees already in place.

CONSTITUTIONAL PROPOSALS

* * *

2. *Public services of the Federal government*
   - The government of Canada should provide public services in both English and French and any person should have the right to communicate with the federal government in either English or French.

* * *

4. *Education*
   - Each child of the French-speaking or English-speaking minority should be entitled,

wherever numbers warrant, to an education in his or her language in the primary and the secondary schools in any province.

* * *

5. *Language obligations of the provinces*
   - Any province may take on language obligations similar to those of the federal government.

– pp.17–18

Questions
1. Read "Hey Quebec Go Suck a Lemon" in the newspaper extract "Bilingualism: A Dirty Word in the West." For what is Quebec being criticized? Is divorce — or separation — an appropriate solution?

2. "Quebec, you're the embodiment of everything I hate about minority groups." How might the author answer the following question: "What rights ought a minority group to have?" Do you agree with the author?

3. Following a reading of the documents in this section:
   (a) prepare a note in which you attempt to summarize the status of French Canadians outside Quebec;
   (b) prepare a list in which you summarize the complaints that anglophone Canadians have made regarding relations between the English and the French in Canada.

4. Can you or your colleagues suggest any measures which will ease tension between English and French Canadians? Is there anything that your community might do to ease the tension?

5. For what reasons have French Canadians argued that "bilingual schools" lead to assimilation? Do you agree?